William Livingston Alden

Christopher Columbus (1440-1506) the first American Citizen

William Livingston Alden

Christopher Columbus (1440-1506) the first American Citizen

ISBN/EAN: 9783337024307

Printed in Europe, USA, Canada, Australia, Japan

Cover: Foto ©ninafisch / pixelio.de

More available books at **www.hansebooks.com**

LIVES OF AMERICAN WORTHIES

CHRISTOPHER COLUMBUS
(1440–1506)

*THE FIRST AMERICAN CITIZEN
(BY ADOPTION)*

BY

W. L. ALDEN

NEW YORK
HENRY HOLT AND COMPANY
1881

CHAPTER I.

EARLY YEARS.

CHRISTOPHER COLUMBUS was born at more places and to a greater extent than any other eminent man known to history. He was born at frequent intervals from 1436 to 1446, and at Cogoletto, Genoa, Finale, Oneglia, Savona, Padrello, and Boggiasco. Learned historians have conclusively shown that he was born at each one of the places, and each historian has had him born at a different date from that fixed upon by a rival historian. To doubt their demonstrations would be to treat history and historians with gross irreverence, and would evince a singular lack of business tact on the part of one proposing to add another to the various histories of Columbus.

Perhaps the majority of people believe that Columbus was born exclusively at

Cogoletto; but no one retains that belief after having once visited Cogoletto, and drank the painfully sour wine produced at that wretched little village. It is true that Mr. Tennyson, who remarks that he once

"Stay'd the wheels at Cogoletto,
And drank, and loyally drank, to him,"

still believes that it was the birthplace of the great Admiral. But this fact simply shows that Mr. Tennyson drank out of his own flask. Few people who visit Cogoletto take this wise precaution, and the result is that, after drinking to the memory of Columbus, they go on their way firmly convinced that wherever else he was born, he certainly was not born at Cogeletto.

It was the opinion of the late Washington Irving that Genoa was the real birthplace of Columbus. This opinion was what might have been expected from a man of such unfailing good taste.

The production of infants is to this day one of the leading industries of Genoa, and as it is a large and beautiful city, we cannot do better than to adopt Mr. Irving's opinion that it was Columbus's favorite birthplace. At the same time we might as well select the year 1436 as the year of his birth, with the determination of adhering to it, for it adds much to the symmetry of a biography if the subject thereof is given a definite and fixed birthday.

At his birth Christopher Columbus was simply Cristoforo Colombo, and it was not until he arrived at manhood that he was translated into Latin, in which tongue he has been handed down to the present generation. At a still later period he translated himself into Spanish, becoming thereby Christoval Colon. We can not be too thankful that he was never translated into German, for we could scarcely take pride in a country discovered by one Kolompo.

The father of Columbus was Domenico Colombo, a wool-comber by occupation. Whose wool he combed, and why he combed it, and whether wool-combing is preferable to wool-gathering as an intellectual pursuit, are questions that have never been satisfactorily decided.

Of Mrs. Colombo we simply know that her Christian name was Fontanarossa, or Red Fountain, a name more suitable to a Sioux Indian than a Christian woman, though perhaps, poor creature! it was not her fault.

Young Christopher was at an early age thoughtfully provided with two younger brothers—who were afterwards very useful to him—and a younger sister. The former were Giacomo, afterward known as Diego, and Bartolommeo, who has been translated into English as Bartholomew. The sister does not appear to have had any name, though her mother might have spared three or four syllables of her own name without feeling the loss of them. This anonymous sister married one Giacomo Bavarello, and promptly vanished into an obscurity that history cannot penetrate.

From his earliest years Christopher was an unusual and remarkable boy. One day when he was about six years of age he was sent by his mother, early in the morning, to the store to purchase a pound of "blueing" for washing purposes. The morning grew to noon, and the afternoon waned until evening—processes which are not peculiar to the climate of Genoa—but the boy did not return, and his mother was unable to wash the family clothes. The truant had forgotten all about the "blueing," and was spending the entire day in company with the McGinnis boys, watching a base-ball match in the City Hall Park between the Genoese Nine and the Red-legs of Turin. At dusk he returned, and his broken-hearted mother handed him over to his stern father, who invited him into the woodshed. As Christopher was removing his coat and loosening his other garments so as to satisfy his father that he had no shingles or school-atlases concealed about his person, he said :

"Father, I stayed to witness that baseball match, not because of a childish curiosity, nor yet because I had any money on the game, but solely in order to study the flight of the ball, hoping thereby to obtain some hints as to the law of projectiles that would enable me to improve the science of gunnery, which is now by no means in an advanced state. If, in view of these circumstances, you still think me worthy of punishment, I will submit with all the fortitude I can summon."

The father, deeply moved at this frank confession, wore out two apple-tree switches in connection with his son, and informed him that if he ever went with those McGinnis boys again he would "let him know."

At another time, when Christopher was about eight years old, his father sent him to a news company's office to get the last number of the *Wool-Combers' Trade Review;* but, as before, the boy failed to return, and after a prolonged search was given up as lost, and his parents decided that he had been run over by the horse-cars. Late in the evening Christopher was detected in the act of trying to sneak into the house through the kitchen windows, and was warmly received by his father, who stood him up in the middle of the kitchen, and without releasing his ear, demanded to know what he had to say for himself.

Christopher, with a saddened expression of face, replied:

"Father, I find it a matter of extreme difficulty to depart from the truth, even at this trying moment. Candor compels me to admit that I have spent the day in company with Michael and Patrick McGinnis, in studying the meteorological laws which affect the flight of kites. With the aid of the last number of the *Wool-Combers' Trade Review* and a few sticks, I made a beautiful kite, and I can confidently say that—"

Here the old gentleman, exclaiming, "That will do! Your explanation is worse than your other crime," applied a rattan cane to the future explorer, and afterwards sent him to bed supperless.

There is not a word of truth in these

two anecdotes, but they are introduced in order to afford the reader a slight glimpse of the boyhood of Columbus. They probably compare favorably, in point of veracity, with the average anecdotes of the boyhood of great men, and they show us that even while Columbus was only six and eight years old he was interested in scientific pursuits, and already gave promise of great tediousness. Still, it would be unwise for any one to believe them, and we will pass on to the more prosaic but truthful facts of Columbus's life.

Young Christopher early conceived a prejudice against wool-combing, although it was his father's earnest desire that he should adopt that profession. Fernando Columbus, the son of the admiral, evidently felt ashamed of his noble father's early wool-combing exploits, and says that Domenico Colombo, so far from desiring his son to comb wool, sent him at the age of thirteen to the University of Pavia to study navigation, with a view of ultimately sending him to sea. Now, although the

United States Government does undertake to teach seamanship with the aid of text-books to young men at the Annapolis Naval Academy, the idea that a young man could become a sailor without going to sea had never occurred to the Genoese, and old Domenico never could have been stupid enough to send his son to the Pavia University with the expectation that he would graduate with the marine degree of "A. B." Undoubtedly Christopher went to Pavia, but it is conceded that he remained there a very short time. If we suppose that, instead of studying his Livy, his Anabasis, and his Loomis's Algebra, he spent his time in reading Marryat's sea stories, and dime novels illustrative of piracy, we can understand why his university course came to a sudden end, and why Domenico remarked to his friends that Christopher studied navigation while at Pavia.

We are told that from his earliest years Christopher desired to be a sailor. We also know that at that period the Mediterranean swarmed with pirates. From these two facts any modern boy with sufficient reasoning powers to be able to put a dog, a string, and a tin can together, will deduce the conclusion that Christopher Columbus must have wanted to be a pirate. As to this there can be but little doubt. When he left Pavia and returned home to comb the paternal wool, he was doubtless fully determined to run away at the earliest opportunity, and become a Red Revenger of the seas.

With this clue, we can readily find in the conduct of the astute Domenico a wise determination to effect a compromise with his adventurous son. He did not want to be the father of a Red Revenger, but he knew that he could not compel his son to comb wool. He therefore induced him to consent to go to sea as a scourge and enemy of pirates; and accordingly in his fourteenth year young Christopher went to sea on board a vessel commanded by a distant relative, who was at one time an admiral in the Genoese service. In what capacity he shipped, whether as a first-class or a second-class boy, or as an acting third assistant cook, or an ordinary cabin-boy, we do not know. Fernando Columbus preserves a discreet silence as to this matter, and as to the first voyage of his father generally. Of course this silence means something, and perhaps Christopher had good reasons for never speaking of the voyage even to his son. Probably he was deathly sea-sick, and in that condition was severely kicked for not being able to lay his hand at a moment's warning upon the starboard main-top-gallant-studding-sail tripping-line, or other abstruse rope. At all events, he always abstained from telling stories beginning, "I reck'lect on my first v'yge;" and we may be sure that he would never have put such an unseamanlike constraint upon his tongue unless he knew that the less he said about that voyage the better.

He had been a sailor for some years when he joined a vessel forming part of an expedition fitted out in Genoa in 1459 by a certain Duke of Calabria named John of Anjou, who wanted to steal the kingdom of Naples in order to give it to his father, René, Count of Provence. So pious a son naturally commanded universal respect, and Genoa provided him with ships and lent him money. The expedition was very large, and the old Admiral Colombo, with whom Christopher sailed, probably commanded the Genoese contingent. The fleet cruised along the Neapolitan coast, and sailed in and out the Bay of Naples any number of times, but owing to a fear of the extortions of the Neapolitan hack-drivers and *valets-de-place*, there seems to have been no attempt made to land at Naples. For four years John of Anjou persevered in trying to conquer Naples, but in vain ; and at the end of that time he must have had a tremendous bill to pay for his Genoese ships.

While engaged in this expedition, Christopher was sent in command of a vessel to Tunis, where he was expected to capture a hostile galley. Carefully reading up his

"Midshipman Easy" and his "Blunt's Coast Pilot," he set sail; but on reaching the island of San Pedro, which can easily be found on any map where it is mentioned by name, he learned that there were also in the harbor of Tunis two ships and a carrick; whereupon his crew remarked that they did not propose to attack an unlimited quantity of vessels, but that if Columbus would put into Marseilles and lay in a few more ships to accompany them, they would gladly cut out all the vessels at Tunis. Columbus was determined not to go to Marseilles,—though he does not definitely say that he owed money to the keeper of a sailor boarding-house there,—but he was unable to shake the resolution of his crew. He therefore pretended to yield to their wishes and set sail again, ostensibly for Marseilles. The next morning, when the crew came on deck, they found themselves near the Cape of Carthagena, and perceived that their wily commander had deceived them.

This story is told by Columbus himself,

and it awakens in the mind of the intelligent reader some little doubt of the narrator's veracity. In the first place, he admits that he deceived his sailors, and hence we have no certainty that he was not trying to deceive the public when telling the story of the alleged deception. In the second place, it is scarcely probable that all the crew promptly "turned in" at sunset, leaving Columbus himself at the wheel; but unless this was done, the compass or the stars must have told them that the ship was not laying the proper course for Marseilles. Finally, Columbus, in his exultation at having deceived his crew, does not so much as mention Tunis, or the hostile vessels which it was his duty to attack, nor does he tell us what business he had at the Cape of Carthagena. We are thus justified in assuming that the story is not entirely credible. Years afterward, on his first transatlantic voyage, Columbus deceived his men concerning the number of leagues they had sailed, and this exploit was so warmly commended by his admirers that he may have been tempted to remark that he always made a point of deceiving sailors, and may thereupon have invented this earlier instance as a case in point. Still, let us not lightly impugn his veracity. Perhaps he really did tell the truth and deceive his sailors ; but whether he did or not, we should still remember that many of us are merely human, and that had we been in the place of Columbus we might have said and done a variety of different things.

What became of Columbus during several subsequent years, we have no trustworthy account. In all probability he continued to follow the sea, and perhaps caught up with it now and then. We know, however, that at one time he commanded a galley belonging to a squadron under the command of Colombo the Younger, a son of the Colombo with whom Christopher sailed in the Neapolitan expedition. This squadron, falling in with a Venetian fleet somewhere off the Portuguese coast, immediately attacked it,

Venice and Genoa being at that time at war. In the course of the battle the galley of Columbus was set on fire, and as he had no available small-boats—a fact which must forever reflect disgrace upon the Genoese Navy Department—he was compelled to jump overboard with all his crew. He seems to have lost all interest in the battle after the loss of his galley, and he therefore decided to go ashore. He was six miles from land, but with the help of an oar which he put under his breast he swam ashore without difficulty, and when we consider that he was dressed in a complete suit of armor, it is evident that he must have been a very fine swimmer.

It should be mentioned that, although this story is told by Fernando Columbus, certain carping critics have refused to believe it, on the paltry pretext that, inasmuch as the naval fight in question took place several years after Columbus is known to have taken up his residence in Portugal, he could not have landed in that country for the first time immediately after the battle. This is mere trifling. If Columbus could swim six miles in a suit of heavy armor, and, in all probability, with his sword in one hand and his speaking-trumpet in the other, he could easily have performed the simpler feat of residing in Portugal several years before he reached that country. The truth is, that historians are perpetually casting doubt upon all legends of any real merit or interest. They have totally exploded the story of Washington and the cherry-tree, and they could not be expected to concede that Fernando Columbus knew more about his father than persons living and writing four hundred years later could know. As to Columbus's great swimming feat, they have agreed to disbelieve the whole story, and of course the public agrees with them.

CHAPTER II.

FIRST PLANS OF EXPLORATION.

IT is at Lisbon that we are able for the first time to put our finger decisively upon Columbus. The stray glimpses which we catch of him before that time, whether at Genoa, Pavia, Naples, or Cape Carthagena, are fleeting and unsatisfactory; his trustworthy biography begins with his residence at Lisbon. He reached there, we do not know by what route, in the year 1470, having no money and no visible means of support. Instead of borrowing money and buying an organ, or calling on the leader of one of the Lisbon political "halls" and obtaining through his influence permission to set up a peanut stand, he took a far bolder course—he married. Let it not be supposed that he represented himself to be an Italian count, and thereby won the hand of an ambitious

Portuguese girl. The fact that he married the daughter of a deceased Italian navigator proves that he did not resort to the commonplace devices of the modern Italian exile. Doña Felipa di Perestrello was not only an Italian, and as such could tell a real count from a Genoese sailor without the use of litmus paper or any other chemical test, but she was entirely without money and, viewed as a bride, was complicated with a mother-in-law. Thus it is evident that Columbus did not engage in matrimony as a fortune-hunter, and that he must have married Doña Felipa purely because he loved her. We may explain in the same way her acceptance of the penniless Genoese; and the fact that they lived happily together—if Fernando Columbus is to be believed—makes it clear that neither expected anything from the other, and hence neither was disappointed.

The departed navigator, Di Perestrello, had been in the service of the Portuguese king, and had accumulated a large quantity of maps and charts, which his widow inherited. She does not appear to have objected to her daughter's marriage, but the depressed state of Columbus's fortunes at this period is shown by the fact that he and his wife went to reside with his mother-in-law, where he doubtless learned that fortitude and dignity when exposed to violence and strong language for which he afterwards became renowned. Old Madame Perestrello did him one really good turn by presenting him with the maps, charts, and log-books of her departed husband, and this probably suggested to him the idea which he proceeded to put into practice, of making and selling maps.

Map-making at that time offered a fine field to an imaginative man, and Columbus was not slow to cultivate it. He made beautiful charts of the Atlantic Ocean, putting Japan, India, and other desirable Asiatic countries on its western shore, and placing quantities of useful islands where he considered that they would do the most good. These maps may possibly have been somewhat inferior in breadth of imagination to an average *Herald* map, but they were far superior in beauty; and the array of novel animals with which the various continents and large islands were sprinkled made them extremely attractive. The man who bought one of Columbus's maps received his full money's worth, and what with map-selling, and occasional sea voyages to and from Guinea at times when Madame Perestrello became rather too free in the use of the stove-lid, Columbus managed to make a tolerably comfortable living.

The island of Porto Santo, then recently discovered, lay in the track of vessels sailing between Portugal and Guinea, and must have attracted the attention of Columbus while engaged in the several voyages which he made early in his married life.

It so happened that Doña Felipa came into possession, by inheritance, of a small property in Porto Santo, and Columbus thereupon abandoned Lisbon and with his family took up his residence on that island. Here he met one Pedro Correo, a bold sailor and a former governor of Porto Santo, who was married to Doña Felipa's sister. Columbus and Correo soon became warm friends, and would sit up together half the night, talking about the progress of geographical discovery and the advantages of finding some nice continent full of gold and at a great distance from the widow Perestrello.

At that time there were certain unprincipled mariners who professed to have discovered meritorious islands a few hundred miles west of Portugal; and though we know that these imaginative men told what was not true, Columbus may have supposed that their stories were not entirely without a basis of truth. King Henry of Portugal, who died three years after Columbus arrived at Lisbon, had a passion for new countries, and the fashion which he set of fitting out exploring expeditions continued to prevail after his death.

There is no doubt that there was a general feeling, at the period when Columbus and Correo lived at Porto Santo, that the discovery of either a continent on the western shore of the Atlantic, or a new route to China, would meet a great popular want. Although the Portuguese had sailed as far south as Cape Bojador, they believed that no vessel could sail any further in that direction without meeting with a temperature so great as to raise the water of the ocean to the boiling-point, and it was thus assumed that all future navigators desirous of new islands and continents must search for them in the west. The more Columbus thought of the matter, the more firmly he became convinced that he could either discover valuable islands by sailing due west, or that at all events he could reach the coast of Japan, China, or India; and that it was clearly the duty of somebody to supply him with ships and money and put him in command of an exploring expedition. With this view Correo fully coincided, and Columbus made up his mind that he would call on a few respectable kings and ask them to fit out such an expedition.

Fernando Columbus informs us that his father based his conviction that land could be found by sailing in a westerly direction, upon a variety of reasons. Although many learned men believed that the earth was round, the circumference of the globe was then unknown; and as every one had therefore a right to call it what he chose, Columbus assumed that it was comparatively small, and that the distance from the Cape Verde Islands eastward to the western part of Asia was fully two thirds of the entire circumference. He also assumed that the remaining third consisted in great part of the eastern portion of Asia, and that hence the distance across the Atlantic, from Portugal to Asia, was by no means great. In support of this theory he recalled the alleged fact that various strange trees and bits of wood, hewn after a fashion unknown in Europe, had from time to time been cast on the European shores, and must have come out of the unknown west.

This theory, founded as it was upon

gratuitous assumptions, and supported by driftwood of uncertain origin and doubtful veracity, was regarded by Columbus as at least the equal of the binomial theorem in credibility, and he felt confident that the moment he should bring it to the attention of an enterprising king, that monarch would instantly present him with a fleet and make him Governor-General of all lands which he might discover.

It was the invariable custom of Columbus to declare that his chief reason for desiring to discover new countries was, that he might carry the Gospel to the pagan inhabitants thereof, and also find gold enough to fit out a new crusade for the recovery of the Holy Sepulchre. Whether old Pedro Correo winked when Columbus spoke in this pious strain, or whether Doña Felipa, with the charming frankness of her sex, remarked "fiddlesticks!" we shall never know.

Perhaps Columbus really thought that he wanted to dispense the Gospel and fight the Mahometans, and that he did not care a straw about becoming a great explorer and having the State capital of Ohio named for him; but his fixed determination not to carry a particle of Gospel to the smallest possible pagan, except upon terms highly advantageous to his pocket and his schemes of personal aggrandizement, is scarcely reconcilable with his pious protestations. His own church decided, not very long ago, that his moral character did not present available materials for the manufacture of a saint, and it is only too probable that the church was right.

It is a curious illustration of the determination of his biographers to prove him an exceptionally noble man, that they dwell with much emphasis upon his stern determination not to undertake any explorations except upon his own extravagant terms. To the unprejudiced mind his conduct might seem that of a shrewd and grasping man, bent upon making a profitable speculation. The biographers, however, insist that it was the conduct of a great and noble nature, caring for nothing except geographical discovery and the conversion of unlimited heathen.

About this time Columbus is believed to have written a great many letters to various people, asking their candid opinion upon the propriety of discovering new continents or new ways to old Asiatic countries. Paulo Toscanelli, of Florence, a leading scientific person, sent him, in answer to one of his letters, a map of the Atlantic and the eastern coast of Asia, which displayed a bolder imagination than Columbus had shown in any of his own maps, and which so delighted him that he put it carefully away, to use in case his dream of exploration should be realized. Toscanelli's map has proved to be of much more use to historians than it was to Columbus, for the letter in which it was enclosed was dated in the year 1474, and it thus gives us the earliest date at which we can feel confident Columbus was entertaining the idea of his great voyage.

How long Columbus resided at Porto Santo we have no means of knowing;

neither do we know why he left that place. It is certain, however, that he returned to Lisbon either before or very soon after the accession of King John II. to the Portuguese throne, an event which took place in 1481. Meanwhile, as we learn from one of his letters, he made a voyage in 1477 to an island which his biographers have agreed to call Iceland, although Columbus lacked inclination—or perhaps courage—to call it by that name. He says he made the voyage in February, and he does not appear to have noticed that the water was frozen. The weak point in his narrative—provided he really did visit Iceland—is his omission to mention how he warmed the Arctic ocean so as to keep it free of ice in February. Had he only given us a description of his sea-warming method, it would have been of inestimable service to the people of Iceland, since it would have rendered the island easily accessible at all times of the year, and it would also have materially lessened the difficulty which explorers find in sailing to the North Pole.

It is probable that Columbus visited some warmer and easier island than Iceland— say one of the Hebrides. In those days a voyage from southern Europe to Iceland would have been a remarkable feat, and Columbus would not have failed to demand all the credit due him for so bold an exploit.

The immediate predecessor of King John —King Alfonso—preferred war to exploration, and as he was occupied during the latter part of his reign in a very interesting war with Spain, it is improbable that Columbus wasted time in asking him to fit out a transatlantic expedition. There is a rumor that, prior to the accession of King John II., Columbus applied to Genoa for assistance in his scheme of exploration, but the rumor rests upon no evidence worth heeding.

Genoa, as every one knows, was then a republic. It needed all its money to pay the expenses of the administration party at elections, to improve its inland harbors and subterranean rivers, and to defray the cost of postal routes in inaccessible parts of the country. Had Columbus asked for an appropriation, the Genoese politicians would have denounced the folly and wickedness of squandering the people's money on scientific junketing expeditions, and would have maintained that a free and enlightened republic ought not to concern itself with the effete and monarchical countries of Asia, to which Columbus was anxious to open a new route.

Moreover, Columbus had been absent from Genoa for several years. He had no claims upon any of the Genoese statesmen, and was without influence enough to carry his own ward. An application of any sort coming from such a man would have been treated with deserved contempt; and we may be very sure that, however much Columbus may have loved the old Genoese flag and desired an appropriation, he had far too much good sense to dream of asking any favors from his fellow-countrymen. Undoubtedly he was as anxious to start in search of America while he lived at

Porto Santo as he was at a later period, but he knew that only a king would feel at liberty to use public funds in what the public would consider a wild and profitless expedition; and as there was no king whom he could hope to interest in his scheme, he naturally waited until a suitable king should appear.

The death of Alfonso provided him with what he imagined would prove to be a king after his own heart, for King John was no sooner seated on the throne than he betrayed an abnormal longing for new countries by sending explorers in search of Prester John.

This Prester John was believed to be a Presbyterian deacon who ruled over a civilized and Christian kingdom which he kept concealed either about his person or in some out-of-the-way part of the world. The wonderful credulity of the age is shown by this belief in a Presbyterian king whom no European had ever seen, and in a kingdom of which no man knew the situation. It ought to have occurred to the Portuguese king that, even if he could find this mythical monarch, he would not take any real pleasure in his society, unless he were to burn him. King John II. was a pious Roman Catholic, and, next to a Methodist, a Presbyterian king would have been about the most uncongenial acquaintance he could have made. Nevertheless, this Presbyterian myth was indirectly of great service to Columbus.

King John, in order to facilitate his search for Prester John, asked a scientific commission to invent some improvements in navigation, the result of which was the invention of the astrolabe, a sort of rudimentary quadrant, by means of which a navigator could occasionally find his latitude. This invention was hardly inferior in value to that of the compass, and it is generally said to have provided Columbus with the means of finding his way across the Atlantic and back to Europe.

Next to the discovery of Prester John, the Portuguese king desired to discover a route by sea to India. He believed with his deceased grand-uncle, Prince Henry, that Africa could be circumnavigated— provided the circumnavigators could avoid being boiled alive south of Cape Bojador —and that a road to India could thus be found. It was manifest that he was just the sort of monarch for Columbus's purposes. He was so anxious to make discoveries that he would have been delighted even to find a Presbyterian. He was particularly bent upon finding a route to India, and he was only twenty-five years old. He was the very man to listen to a solemn and oppressive mariner with his pockets full of maps and his mind full of the project for a transatlantic route to India. Columbus was now about forty-six years old, and his beard was already white. He had dwelt so long upon the plan of crossing the Atlantic that he resembled the Ancient Mariner in his readiness to button-hole all sorts of people and compel them to listen to his project. Mrs. Perestrello appears to have been safely dead at this time, and Pedro Correo had probably been talked to death by his relentless brother-in-law. Still, Columbus was as anxious to carry out his plan as ever. He marked young King John as his prey, and finally obtained an audience with him.

CHAPTER III.

IN SEARCH OF A PATRON.

WE have two accounts of the interview between Columbus and the King—one written by Fernando Columbus, and the other by Juan de Barros, an eminent geographer. Fernando says that the King listened with great delight to the project of Columbus, and only refrained from instantly giving him the command of an expedition because he did not feel ready to consent to Columbus's conditions. De Barros says that King John finally professed that he approved of Columbus's views merely to get rid of that persistent mariner.

However this may be, the King referred the whole matter to a committee, with power to send for maps and things. The committee consisted of two geographers—who of course hated Columbus with true scientific hatred—and the King's confessor, the Bishop of Ceuta. It did not take very long for the committee to decide that Columbus was a preposterous person, and that his project was impracticable. The King then referred the matter to his council, where it was hotly debated. The Bishop of Ceuta took the broad, general ground that exploration was an idle and frivolous occupation; that no men of sense wanted any new countries; and that if the King must have amusement, the best thing he could do would be to make war upon the Moors.

Don Pedro de Meneses replied with much vigor, hurling back the Bishop's accusations against exploration, and nailing his reverence's misstatements as boldly as if the two were rival Congressmen. As for himself, Don Pedro said, he liked new continents, and believed that Portugal could not have too many of them. He considered Columbus a great man, and felt that it would be a precious privilege for other people to aid in the proposed transatlantic scheme.

Nevertheless, the council decided against it, much, we are told, to the King's disappointment.

The Bishop of Ceuta, in spite of his remarks at the meeting of the committee, evidently thought there might be something in Columbus's plan after all. He therefore proposed to the King that Columbus should be induced to furnish written proposals and specifications for the discovery of transatlantic countries, and that with the help of the information thus furnished the King should secretly send a vessel to test the practicability of the scheme. This was done, but the vessel returned after a few days, having discovered nothing but water.

As soon as Columbus heard of this trick he became excessively angry, and resolved that King John should never have a square foot of new territory, nor a solitary heathen soul to convert, if he could help it. Accordingly, he broke off his acquaintance with the King, and proposed to leave Lisbon, in the mean time sending his brother Bartholomew to England to ask if the English King would like to order a supply of new islands or a transatlantic continent. His wife had already succumbed to her husband's unremitting conversation concerning explorations, and died, doubtless with much resignation. Madame Perestrello, Pedro Correo, and Mrs. Columbus were probably only a few of the many unhappy Portuguese who suffered from the fatal conversational powers of Columbus, and Portugal may have become rather an unsafe place for him. This would account for the stealthy way in which he left that kingdom, and is at least as probable as the more common theory that he ran away to escape his creditors.

It was in the year 1484 that Columbus, accompanied by his son Diego, shook the dust of Portugal from his feet and climbed over the back-fence into Spain, in the dead of night, instead of openly taking the regular mail-coach. The King of England had refused to listen to Bartholomew's proposals, and King John had been guilty of conduct unbecoming a monarch and a gentleman. This may have given Columbus a prejudice against kings, for he made his next applications to the Dukes of Medina Sidonia and Medina Celi—two noblemen residing in the south of Spain.

Medina Sidonia listened to Columbus with much interest, and evidently regarded him as an entertaining kind of lunatic; but after a time he became seriously alarmed at the Italian's inexhaustible capacity for talk, and courteously got rid of him before sustaining any permanent injury. The Duke of Medina Celi was a braver man, and not only invited Columbus to come and stay at his house, but actually spoke of lending him ships and money. He changed his mind, however, and told Columbus that he really could not take the liberty of fitting out an expedition which ought to be fitted out by a king. Columbus then remarked that he would step over to France and speak to the French King about it; whereupon the Duke hastily wrote to Queen Isabella, of Castile and Aragon, mentioning that he had a mariner of great merit in his house, whom she really ought to see. The Queen graciously wrote, requesting the Duke to forward his ancient mariner to the royal palace at Cordova, which he accordingly did, furnishing Columbus at the same time with a letter of introduction to Her Majesty.

Spain was then merely a geographical expression. Ferdinand, King of Aragon, had recently married Isabella, Queen of Castile, and their joint property was called the Kingdom of Castile and Aragon; for, inasmuch as the Moors still ruled over the southern part of the peninsula, it would have been indelicate for Ferdinand and his queen to pretend that they were the monarchs of all Spain.

When Columbus reached Cordova he found that their majesties were on the point of marching against the Moors, and had no time to listen to any plans of exploration. Before starting, however, the Queen deposited Columbus with Alonzo de Quintanilla, the treasurer of Castile, and, we may presume, took a receipt for him. Quintanilla, an affable old gentleman, was much pleased with Columbus, and soon became a warm advocate of his theories. He introduced the navigator to several influential friends, and Columbus passed the summer and winter very pleasantly.

At Cordova he also met a young person named Beatrix Enriquez, to whom he became much attached, and who was afterward the mother of his son Fernando. She probably had her good qualities; but as Columbus was so much preoccupied with his transatlantic projects he forgot to marry her, and hence she is scarcely the sort of young person to be introduced into a virtuous biography.

During the same winter the King and Queen held their court at Salamanca, after having made a very brilliant foray into the Moorish territory, and having also suppressed a rebellion in their own dominions. Columbus went to Salamanca, where he made the acquaintance of Pedro Gonsalvez de Mendoza, the Cardinal-Archbishop of Toledo, who was decidedly the most influential man in the kingdom. When Columbus first mentioned his project, the Cardinal told him the Scriptures asserted that the earth was flat, and that it would be impious for him to prove it was round; but Columbus soon convinced him that the Church would be greatly benefited by the discovery of gold-mines all ready to be worked, and of heathen clamoring to be converted, and thus successfully reconciled science and religion. The Cardinal heartily entered into his scheme, and soon obtained for him an audience with the King.

Columbus says that on this occasion he spoke with an eloquence and zeal that he had never before displayed. The King listened with great fortitude, and when Columbus temporarily paused in his oration had still strength enough left to dismiss him with a promise to refer the matter to a scientific council. In pursuance of this promise he directed Fernando de Talavera, the Queen's confessor, to summon the most learned men of the kingdom to examine Columbus thoroughly and decide upon the feasibility of his plan. As for the Queen, she does not appear to have been present at the audience given to Columbus, either because her royal husband considered the female mind incapable of wrestling with geography, or because he did not think her strong enough to endure Columbus's conversation.

The scientific Congress met at Salamanca without any unnecessary delay, and as few people except priests had any learning whatever at that period, the Congress consisted chiefly of different kinds of priests. They courteously gave Columbus his innings, and listened heroically to his interminable speech, after which they proceeded to demonstrate to him that he was little better than a combined heretic and madman. They quoted the Bible and the opinions of the Fathers of the church in support of the theory that the earth was flat instead of round.

When Columbus in his turn proved that the Bible and the Fathers must be understood in a figurative sense, the priests then took the ground that if the world was round, Columbus could not carry enough provisions with him to enable him to sail around it, and that he could not sail back from his alleged western continent unless his vessels could sail up-hill.

Gradually the more sensible members of the congress came to the conclusion that it would be better to agree to everything Columbus might propose, rather than listen day after day to his appalling eloquence. Still, the majority were men of ascetic lives and great physical endurance, and they showed no disposition to yield to argument or exhaustion. The sessions of the Congress were thus prolonged from day to day, and Columbus was kept in a painful state of suspense. Little did he imagine that in the land which he was destined to discover, another Congress would meet, not quite four hundred years later, and would even surpass the Congress of Salamanca in the tediousness and uselessness of its debates.

CHAPTER IV.

HE RECEIVES HIS COMMISSION.

THE spring of 1487 arrived, and the Council of Salamanca had not yet made its report. The King and Queen, who seem to have required an annual Moorish war in order to tone up their systems, set out to besiege Malaga early in the spring, taking De Talavera with them, so that he might be on hand to confess the Queen in case she should find it desirable to commit a few sins and require subsequent absolution. The departure of De Talavera interrupted the sittings of the Council, and left Columbus without any regular occupation. During the siege of Malaga he was more than once summoned to the camp, ostensibly to confer with the court upon his famous project, but the proposed conferences never took place. He became so tired of the suspense in which he was kept, that he wrote to King John of Portugal, giving him one more chance to accede to his transatlantic plans. Not only did King John answer his letter and ask him to come to Lisbon, but King Henry VII. of England also wrote to him, inviting him to come to England and talk the matter over. At least, Columbus says that those two kings wrote to him; though the fact that he did not accept their invitations, but preferred to waste his time in Spain, casts a little doubt upon his veracity. It is certainly improbable that he would have waited for years in the hope of another interview with Ferdinand and Isabella, if at the same time two prominent kings were writing to him and urging him to bring his carpet-bag and make them a nice long visit.

In the spring of 1489 Columbus was summoned to Seville, and was positively assured that this time he should have a satisfactory conference with a new assortment of learned men. But no sooner had he reached Seville than the King and

Queen suddenly remembered that they had not had their usual spring war, and thereupon promptly started to attack the Moors. Columbus went with them, and fought with great gallantry. Probably it was in some measure due to a dread of his awful conversational powers that the Moorish king surrendered, and it is to the honor of the Christian monarchs that they did not abuse their victory by permitting Columbus to talk to the royal prisoner.

Another year passed away, and still Columbus was waiting for a decision upon the feasibility of his plan. In the spring of 1491 he finally became so earnest in demanding a decision, that the King directed De Talavera and his learned friends to make their long-delayed report. They did so, assuring the King that it would be absurd for him to waste any money whatever in attempting to carry out the Italian's utterly ridiculous plan. Still Ferdinand did not care to drive Columbus to despair, but politely informed him that after he should have finished the annual Moorish war upon which he was just about to enter, he would really try to think of the propriety of fitting out an expedition.

Columbus had now been nearly seven years in Spain, waiting for the King to come to a final decision; and this last postponement exhausted his patience. The court had from time to time supplied him with money; but he was not willing to spend his life as a pensioner on the royal bounty, while the western continent was vainly calling to him to come over and discover it. He therefore left Seville, with the resolution to have nothing further to do with Spain, but to proceed to France and try what he could do with the French king.

He seems to have journeyed on foot, for the very next time we hear of him is as a venerable and imposing tramp, accompanied by an unidentified small-boy, and asking for food—presumably buckwheat cakes, and eggs boiled precisely three minutes—at the gate of the convent of Santa Maria de Rabida.

The Prior of the convent, Juan Perez

de Marchena, happened to notice him, and entered into conversation with him. Columbus told him his name, and mentioned that he was on his way to a neighboring town to find his brother-in-law; from which we learn that four hundred years ago the myth of a brother-in-law in the next town was as familiar to the tramps of that period as it is to those of the present day. As the Prior listened to this story without making any remarks upon its improbability, Columbus was tempted to launch into general conversation, and in a few moments told him all about his desire to find a transatlantic continent, and his intention of offering to the King of France the privilege of assisting him.

Doubtless the good friar found his convent life rather monotonous, and perceiving vast possibilities of conversation in Columbus, he determined to ask him to spend the night with him. Columbus, of course, accepted the invitation, and, the Prior sending for the village doctor, the three spent a delightful evening.

The next day both the Prior and the doctor agreed that Columbus was really a remarkable man, and that it would be disgraceful if the French king were to be allowed to assist in discovering a new continent. The Prior sent for several ancient mariners residing in the neighboring port of Palos, and requested them to give their opinion of the matter. With one accord, they supported the scheme of Columbus with arguments the profundity of which Captain Bunsby himself might have envied; and one Martin Alonzo Pinzon, in particular, was so enthusiastic that he offered to pay the expenses of Columbus while making another application to the court, and to furnish and take command of a vessel in case the application should be successful.

The religious interests of the convent must have suffered somewhat from the Prior's geographical soirées. It must have required a great deal of punch to bring those ancient seafaring men into unanimity upon any subject, and the extent to which Columbus unquestionably availed himself of the opportunity for unrestrained conversation must have left the Prior no time whatever for prayers. He may have excused himself to his own conscience by pretending that to listen to Columbus was a means of mortifying the flesh; but, plausible as this excuse was, it could not justify the introduction of punch, seafaring men, and village doctors into a professedly religious house.

The upshot of the matter was, that the Prior resolved to write a letter to the Queen, and old Sebastian Rodriguez, a veteran sailor, staked the future integrity of his personal eyes upon his delivery of the letter into the hands of Isabella. The Prior had been formerly the Queen's confessor, and of course he knew how to awaken her interest by little allusions to the sinful secrets that she had committed to his holy keeping.

The letter was written, and in two weeks' time Rodriguez brought back an answer summoning the Prior to court. The good old man was overjoyed, and immediately went to Santa Fé, where the King and Queen were stopping, on their way to another Moorish war. When he was admitted to the Queen's presence, he conducted himself with so much discretion, and made so favorable an impression, that Isabella gave him the magnificent sum of twenty thousand maravedies, and told him to hand it over to Columbus, and to send that persistent navigator immediately to her. It is somewhat of a disappointment to learn that the twenty thousand maravedies were in reality worth only seventy-two dollars; still they were enough to enable Columbus to buy a mule and a new spring overcoat, and thus to appear at court in an impressive manner.

The particular Moorish war upon which the King and Queen were then engaged was the very last one of the series, and it was confessedly of so much importance that Columbus did not try to obtain an audience until it was finished. In the mean time he lived with his old friend Alonzo de Quintanella, the treasurer.

At last the day came when, the war being ended, Columbus was summoned to meet a committee of which De Talavera appears to have been the chairman. This time the feasibility of his scheme was admitted, and it only remained to settle the terms upon which he would agree to furnish Spain with new continents. Though Columbus expected to reach the eastern coast of Asia by crossing the Atlantic, that part of Asia was so wholly unknown to Europeans, that its discovery by means of a transatlantic voyage would have enabled the discoverer to take possession of it as a new continent; and it was hence quite proper for Columbus to speak of discovering a new world when he was really intending to discover the eastern half of what we now call the Old world.

It is all very well to have a good opinion of one's self, but Columbus really did put what seems to unprejudiced people a tremendous price upon his services. Not only did he demand one tenth of whatever profits might be derived from his discoveries, but he insisted that he should be made an admiral, and viceroy over every country that he might discover. One of the committee justly remarked that the proposed arrangement was one by which Columbus had everything to gain and nothing to lose, and that if he made no discoveries whatever he would still be a Spanish admiral, and would outrank scores of deserving officers who had spent their lives in the service of their country. Columbus thereupon modified his terms by consenting to take only an eighth of the profits, and to furnish one eighth of the expenses.

It so happened that some member of the committee knew that one eighth was more, instead of less, than one tenth. We need not wonder, therefore, that the committee reported that the terms proposed were inadmissible. De Talavera told the Queen that he had met with a good deal of "cheek" in his time, but the cheek of Columbus was positively monumental, and that nature designed him not for an explorer but for a life-insurance agent.

The result was that the Queen decided to have no more to do with the affair, and Columbus, in a tremendous rage, climbed upon his mule and rode out of Santa Fè, remarking that he wouldn't discover a continent for the Spanish monarchs if continents were as thick as blackberries. He furthermore declared that he would go straight to France and make a contract with the French king, and that the Spaniards would never cease to regret their short-sighted economy.

As the extremity of the Columbian mule vanished through the city gate, Luis de St. Angel, treasurer of the Church funds of the kingdom of Aragon, and the much-suffering Quintanella—who did not believe that Columbus would really go to France, and were convinced that the true way in which to be permanently rid of him was to send him on his proposed expedition—hastened to the palace, and told the monarchs that they were risking the loss of a new continent because they were afraid to risk two ships and a comparatively small sum of money, and because they hesitated to give the title of Admiral to an explorer who, if he did not succeed, would in all probability never return to Spain.

The Queen was much impressed by this straightforward statement of facts, and admitted that she would like to employ Columbus upon his own terms. The King, instead of saying, "Certainly, my dear; do so, by all means!" began to speak of the emptiness of the treasury and the necessity for economy. Of course this made Isabella indignant, and she rose up and exclaimed, "I will undertake the enterprise in behalf of Castile, and will raise the money if I have to pawn my jewels."

Quintanella and St. Angel applauded this resolution, and the latter offered to advance the necessary money without any security whatever. Inasmuch as the money in St. Angel's hands belonged to Aragon, this was a remarkably neat way of saddling the whole expense upon King Ferdinand's private dominions; and there are few ladies who will not concede that it served the King right.

A messenger was at once sent to recall Columbus, and that astute person, grimly smiling at the success of his threat to go to France, prevailed upon his mule to turn back and reënter Santa Fé. He was immediately given an audience with the Queen, and a contract was drawn up in which his utmost demands were recognized. He was to have a tenth of everything, and to rank with the High Admiral of Castile, while instead of his being required to contribute an eighth of the cost of the expedition, it was simply specified that he might make such a contribution if he should feel so inclined. The contract was signed on the 17th of April, 1492, and Columbus's commission as Admiral and Viceroy was immediately made out and given to him.

From 1474 to 1492, or precisely eighteen years, Columbus had been seeking for assistance to cross the Atlantic. During that entire period he was without money, without any visible means of support, and without powerful friends. Nevertheless, he finally obtained from Ferdinand and Isabella a full compliance with demands that to nearly every Spaniard seemed wildly preposterous. To what did he owe his success? It seems very plain that it must have been due to his unparalleled powers of conversation. We know that most of those persons with whom he was on familiar terms when he first conceived his scheme soon died, and the inference that they were talked to death is irresistible. Beyond any doubt, these were only a few of his victims. Columbus talked in Portugal until he was compelled to fly the kingdom, and he talked in Spain until the two monarchs and a few other clear-headed persons felt that if he could be got out of the country by providing him with ships, money, and titles, it must be done. We can readily understand why the news that he was actually about to leave Spain, and to undertake a voyage in the course of which it was universally believed he would be drowned, was received by the Spaniards with unanimous delight. Women wept tears of joy, and strong men went into secluded corners and stood on their heads in wild hilarity. The day of their deliverance was at hand, and the devastating career of the terrible talker was nearly at an end.

CHAPTER V.

HE IS COMMISSIONED, AND SETS SAIL.

ON the 12th of May, 1492, Columbus left Santa Fé for Palos, the seaport from which his expedition was to sail. He left his small-boy, Diego, behind him, as page to Prince Juan, the heir of Castile and Aragon. Diego was the son of his lawful wife, and it is pleasant to find that, in spite of this fact, Columbus still remembered him. His favorite son was of course Fernando, who, with his mother, Beatrix, seems to have been sent away to board in the country during Columbus's absence at sea.

As soon as he arrived at Palos, Columbus called on his worthy friend the Prior, and on the next day the two went to the church of St. George, where the royal order directing the authorities of Palos to supply Columbus with two armed ships, and calling upon everybody to furnish the expedition with all necessary aid, was read aloud by a notary-public. The authorities, as well as the other inhabitants of Palos, were naturally only too glad to do everything in their power to hasten the departure of Columbus; but it was found extremely difficult to procure ships or sailors for the expedition. The merchants very justly said that, much as they might desire to have Columbus drowned, they did not care to furnish ships at their own expense for an enterprise in the interest of all classes of the community. The sailors declared that they were ready to ship for any voyage which might be mentioned, but that it was a little too much to ask them to go to sea with Columbus as their captain, since he would undoubtedly use his authority to compel them to listen to a daily lecture on "Other Continents than Ours," thus rendering their situation far worse than that of ordinary slaves.

The King and Queen, learning of the failure of Columbus to obtain ships and men, and fearing that he might return to court, ordered the authorities of Palos to seize eligible vessels by force, and to kidnap enough sailors to man them. This would probably have provided Columbus with ships and men, had not the short-sighted monarch appointed one Juan de Peñalosa to see that the order was executed, and promised him two hundred maravedies a day until the expedition should be ready. De Peñalosa was perhaps not the intellectual equal of the average American office-holder, but he had sense enough to appreciate his situation, and of course made up his mind that it would take him all the rest of his natural life to see that order carried out. Accordingly, he drew his pay with great vigor and faithfulness, but could not find any ships which, in his opinion, were fit to take part in the proposed expedition. The people soon perceived the state of affairs, and despaired of ever witnessing the departure of Columbus.

Doubtless De Peñalosa would have gone

on for years failing to find the necessary ships, had not two noble mariners resolved to sacrifice themselves on the altar of their country. Martin Alonzo Pinzon and Vincente Yanez Pinzon, his brother, were the two marine patriots in question. They offered a ship and crew, and the magistrates, emulating their patriotism, seized two other ships and ordered them to be fitted for service.

These vessels were under one hundred tons' burthen each, and only one of them, the *Santa Maria*, was decked over. In model they resembled the boats carved by small inland boys, and their rig would have brought tears to the eyes of a modern sailor—provided, of course, a way of bringing a modern sailor to Palos to inspect them could have been devised. If we can put any faith in woodcuts, the *Santa Maria* and her consorts were two-masted vessels carrying one or two large square sails on each mast, and remotely resembling dismasted brigs rigged with jury-masts by some passengers from Indiana who had studied rigging and seamanship in Sunday-school books. The pretence that those vessels could ever beat to windward cannot be accepted for a moment. They must have been about as fast and weatherly as a St. Lawrence "pin flat," and in point of safety and comfort they were even inferior to a Staten Island ferry-boat.

The *Pinta* was commanded by Martin Pinzon, and the *Niña* by Vincente Pinzon. No less than four pilots were taken, though how four pilots could have been equally divided among three ships without subjecting at least one pilot to a subdivision that would have seriously impaired his efficiency, can not readily be comprehended. Indeed, no one has ever satisfactorily explained why Columbus wanted pilots, when he intended to navigate utterly unknown seas. It has been suggested that he had bound himself not to talk to an intemperate extent to his officers or men, and that he laid in a supply of private pilots purely for the purpose of talking to them. It is much more probable that a law of compulsory pilotage existed at that time in Spain,—for it was a dark and ignorant age,—and that, inasmuch as Columbus would have had to pay the pilots whether he took them with him or not, he thought he might as well accept their services. Besides, he may have remembered that a vessel rarely runs aground unless she is in charge of a pilot, and hence he may have imagined that pilots possessed a peculiar skill in discovering unexpected shores at unlooked-for moments, and might materially help him in discovering a new continent by running the fleet aground on its coast.

A royal notary was also sent with the expedition, so that if any one should suddenly desire to swear or affirm, as the case might be, it could be done legally. The three vessels carried ninety sailors, and the entire expeditionary force consisted of one hundred and twenty men.

The ship-carpenters and stevedores, doubtless at the instigation of Peñalosa, made all the delay they possibly could, and at the last moment a large number of sailors deserted. Other sailors were procured, and finally evetything was in readiness for the departure of the fleet. On Friday the 3d of August, 1492, Columbus and his officers and men confessed themselves and received the sacrament, after which the expedition put to sea.

In spite of the knowledge that Columbus was actually leaving Spain with a very slight prospect of ever returning, the departure of the ships cast a gloom over Palos. The people felt that to sacrifice one hundred and nineteen lives, with three valuable vessels, was a heavy price to pay, even for permanently ridding Spain of the devastating talker. Still, we are not told that they permitted sentiment to overpower their patriotism, and they were probably sustained by the reflection that it was better that one hundred and nineteen other people should be drowned, than that they themselves should be talked to death.

It is universally agreed that it is impossible not to admire the courage displayed by Columbus and his associates. The ships of the expedition were small and unseaworthy. They were not supplied with ice-houses, hot water, electric bells, saloons amidships where the motion is least perceptible, smoking and bath rooms, or any of the various other devices by which the safety of modern steamships is secured. The crew knew that they were bound to an unknown port, and that if their vessels managed to reach it there was no certainty that they would find any rum. Columbus had employed eighteen years in convincing himself that if he once set sail he would ultimately arrive somewhere; but now that he was finally afloat, his faith must have wavered somewhat. As he was an excellent sailor, he could not but have felt uncomfortable when he remembered that he had set sail on Friday. However, he professed to be in the very best of spirits, and no one can deny that he was as brave as he was tedious.

On the third day out, the *Pinta* unshipped her rudder, and soon after began to leak badly. Her commander made shift partially to repair the disaster to the rudder, but Columbus determined to put into the Canaries, and charter another vessel in her place. He knew that he was then not far from the Canaries, although the pilots, either because their minds were already weakening under the strain of their commander's conversation, or because they were ready to contradict him at every possible opportunity, insisted that the islands were a long way off. Columbus was right, and on the 9th of August they reached the Canaries, where we may suppose the pilots were permitted to go ashore and obtain a little rest.

For three weeks Columbus waited in hopes of finding an available ship, but he was disappointed. The *Pinta* was therefore repaired to some extent, and the *Niña* was provided with a new set of sails. A report here reached Columbus that three Portuguese men-of-war were on their way to capture him—doubtless on the charge of having compassed the death of several Portuguese subjects with violent and prolonged conversation. He therefore set sail at once, and as he passed the volcano, which was then in a state of eruption, the crews were so much alarmed that they were on the point of mutiny. Columbus, however, made them a speech on the origin, nature, and probable object of volcanoes, which soon reduced them to the most abject state of exhaustion.

Nothing was seen of the Portuguese men-of-war, and it has been supposed that some practical joker alarmed the Admiral by filling his mind with visions of hostile ships, when the only Portuguese men-of-war in that part of the Atlantic were the harmless little jelly-fish popularly known by that imposing title.

It was the 6th day of September when the expedition left the Canaries, but owing to a prolonged calm it was not until the 9th that the last of the islands was lost sight of. We can imagine what the devoted pilots must have suffered during those three days in which Columbus had nothing to do but talk; but they were hardy men, and they survived it. They remarked to one another that they could die but once; that care had once killed a vague and legendary cat; and in various other ways tried to reconcile themselves to their fate.

The crew on losing sight of land became, so we are told, utterly cast down, as they reflected upon the uncertainty of ever again seeing a Christian grog-shop, or joining with fair ladies in the cheerful fandango. Mr. Irving says that "rugged seamen shed tears, and some broke into loud lamentation," and that Columbus thereupon made them a long speech in order to reconcile them to their lot. The probability is that Mr. Irving reversed the order of these two events. If Columbus made a long speech to his crew, as he very likely did, there is no doubt that they shed tears, and lamented loudly.

Lest the crew should be alarmed at the distance they were rapidly putting between themselves and the spirituous liquors of Spain, Columbus now adopted the plan of daily falsifying his reckoning. Thus if the fleet had sailed one hundred miles in any given twenty-four hours, he would announce that the distance sailed was only sixty miles. Meanwhile he kept a private log-book, in which he set down the true courses and distances sailed. This system may have answered its purpose, but had the fleet been wrecked, and had the false and the true log-books both fallen into the hands of the underwriters, Columbus would not have recovered a dollar of insurance, and would probably have been indicted for forgery with attempt to lie. The lawyer for the insurance company would have put in evidence the two entries for, let us say, the 10th of September; the one reading, "Wind E.S.E., light and variable; course W. by N.; distance by observation since noon yesterday, 61 miles;" and the other, or true entry, reading, "Wind E.S.E.; course W. by N.; distance by observation since noon yesterday, 117 miles. At

HE IS COMMISSIONED.

seven bells in the morning watch, furled main-top-gallant sails, and put a single reef in all three topsails. This day ends with a strong easterly gale." With such evidence as this, he would easily have proved that Columbus was a desperate villain, who had wrecked his vessels solely to swindle the insurance companies. Thus we see that dishonesty will vitiate the best policy, provided the underwriters can prove it.

It was perhaps this same desire to lead his crew into the belief that the voyage would not be very long, which led Columbus to insert in the sailing directions given to the two Pinzons an order to heave-to every night as soon as they should have sailed seven hundred leagues west of the Canaries. He explained that unless this precaution were taken they would be liable to run foul of China in the night, in case the latter should not happen to have lights properly displayed. This was very thoughtful, but there is no reason to think that it deceived the Pinzons. They knew perfectly well that Columbus had not the least idea of the distance across the Atlantic, and they probably made remarks to one another in regard to the difficulty of catching old birds with chaff, which the Admiral would not have enjoyed had he heard them.

Thus cheerfully cheating his sailors, and conversing with his pilots, Columbus entered upon his voyage. A great many meritorious emotions are ascribed to him by his biographers, and perhaps he felt several of them. We have, however, no evidence on this point, and the probability is that he would not have expressed any feeling but confidence in his success to any person. He had long wanted to sail in quest of new continents, and his wish was now gratified. He ought to have been contented, and it is quite possible that he was.

CHAPTER VI.

THE VOYAGE.

IN those days everybody supposed that the needle always pointed due north. Great was the astonishment of Columbus when, a few days after leaving the Canaries, he noticed what is now called the variation of the compass. Instead of pointing to the north, the needle began to point somewhat to the west of north; and the farther the fleet sailed to the west, the greater became the needle's variation from the hitherto uniform direction of all respectable needles. Of course Columbus at first supposed that his compass was out of order, but he soon found that every compass in the fleet was conducting itself in the same disreputable way. The pilots also noticed the startling phenomenon, and said it was just what they had expected. In seas so remote from the jurisdiction of Spain, who could expect that the laws of Nature would be observed? They did not like to grumble, but still they must say that it was simply impious to sail in regions where even the compass could not tell the truth. But Columbus was not the man to be put to confusion by remarks of this kind. He calmly told the pilots that the compass was all right; it was the North Star that was wrong, and he never had felt much confidence in that star, anyway. Then inviting the pilots to come down into his cabin and take a little—well, lunch, he explained to them with such profound unintelligibility the astronomical habits and customs of the North Star, that they actually believed his explanation of the variation of the compass. There are those who hold that Columbus really believed the North Star was leaving its proper place; but the theory does gross injustice to the splendid mendacity of the Admiral. The man who could coolly assert that if his compass differed from the stars the latter were at fault, deserves the wonder and admiration of even the most skilful editor of a campaign edition of an American party organ.

The sailors would probably have grumbled a good deal about the conduct of the compass had they noticed it; but it does not appear that they had any suspicion that it had become untrustworthy. Besides, the fleet was now fairly in the trade-wind, and very little labor was required in the management of the vessels. The sailors, having little to do, were in good spirits, and began to see signs of land. A large meteor was seen to fall into the sea, and soon after a great quantity of sea-weed was met, among which tunny-fish made their home. The Admiral also caught a small crab. Crabs, tunny-fish, sea-weed, and meteors must have been, in those days, exclusively products of the land; otherwise, there was no reason why Columbus and his men should have regarded them as proofs of the vicinity of land. They did, however, meet with a bird of a variety—so the oldest mariners asserted—that never sleeps except on a good substantial roosting-place. This really did give them some reason to imagine that land was not very far off; but as the result showed, the bird was painfully untrustworthy.

Day after day the so-called signs of land were seen. A large reward was offered to the first person who should see the sought-for continent, and consequently everybody was constantly pretending that a distant cloud or fog-bank was land, and then finding fault with the Admiral because he would not change his course. One day a pair of boobies—a bird singularly misnamed, in view of the fact that it rarely flies out of sight of land—rested in the rigging. Another day three birds of a kind—which, every one knows, were even better than two pairs—came on board one of the ships in the morning, and flew away again at night, and it was the universal opinion that they sang altogether too sweetly for sea-birds; the voices of the gull, the stormy petrel, and the albatross being notoriously far from musical.

After a time these signs ceased to give the crews any comfort. As they forcibly observed, "What is the use of all your signs of land, so long as you don't fetch on your land?" They became convinced that the sea was gradually becoming choked up with sea-weed, and that the fact that the surface of the water remained unruffled, although there was a steady breeze from the east, was proof that something was seriously wrong. We now know that the expedition was in the Sargasso Sea, a region of sea-weed and calms, and that in point of fact Columbus was lucky in not being becalmed for a year or two without any means of bringing his vessels to a more breezy region. This, however, he did not know, and he explained the quiet of the sea by asserting that the fleet was already in the lee of the unseen land.

The men nevertheless continued to be discontented, and declined any longer to believe that land was near. Even the sight of a whale—which, as every one knows, is a land animal—failed to raise their spirits, although Columbus told them that, now that he had seen a whale, he knew they must be very near the shore. The sailors would not listen to his argument, and openly insulted his whale. They said he had brought them to a region where the wind either blew steadily from the east or scarcely blew at all; in either case opposing an insuperable obstacle to sailing back to Spain, for which reason, with the charming consistency of sailors, they wanted to turn back immediately and steer for Palos. Still, they did not break into open mutiny, but confined themselves to discussing the propriety of seizing the vessels, throwing Columbus overboard, and returning to Spain, where they could account for the disappearance of the Admiral by asserting that he had been pushed overboard by the cat, or had been waylaid, robbed, and murdered by the James boys; or by inventing some other equally plausible story. Happily, the wind finally sprang up again, and the sailors, becoming more cheerful, postponed their mutiny.

The typical biographer always begs us to take notice that Columbus must have been a very great man, for the reason that he prosecuted his great voyage in spite of the frequent mutinies of the sailors; and as we shall hereafter see, Columbus was troubled by mutinies during other voyages than his first one. At the present day, however, the ability of a sea-captain would not be estimated by the number of times his crew had mutinied. If Columbus was really an able commander, how did it happen that he ever allowed a mutiny to break out? Very likely his flagship was short of belaying-pins and handspikes, but did not the Admiral wear a sword and carry pistols? and was he not provided with fists and the power to use them? Instead of going on deck at the first sign of mutinous conduct on the part of any one of the crew, and striking terror and discipline into the offender with the first available weapon, he seems to have waited quietly in the cabin until the sailors had thrown off all authority, and then to have gone on deck and induced them to resume work by delivering a lecture on geography and the pleasures of exploration. But we should remember that he was in command of Spanish vessels, and that Spanish views of seamanship and discipline are peculiar.

On the 25th of September, Martin Pinzon, whose vessel happened to be within hailing distance of Columbus, suddenly shouted that he saw land in the southwest, and wanted that reward. The alleged land rapidly became clearly visible, and seemed to be a very satisfactory piece of land, though it was too far off to show any distinctively Japanese, Chinese, or East Indian features. Columbus immediately called his men together, made a prayer, and ordered them to sing a psalm. The fleet then steered toward the supposed land, which soon proved to be an exasperating fog-bank, whereupon the sailors unanimously agreed that Columbus had trifled with the holiest feelings of their nature, and that they could not, with any self-respect, much longer postpone the solemn duty of committing his body to the deep.

About this time a brilliant idea occurred to the Pinzons. It was that the true direction in which to look for land was the south-west, and that Columbus ought to give orders to steer in that direction. As they had no conceivable reason for this belief, and could advance no argument whatever in support of it, they naturally adhered to it with great persistency. Columbus declined to adopt their views—partly because they were the independent views of the Pinzons, and, as is well known, no subordinate officer has any right to independent views, and partly because they were entirely worthless. The Pinzons were therefore compelled to console themselves by remarking that of course the Admiral meant well, but they were sadly afraid he was a grossly incompetent discoverer. On the 7th of October the spirits of the sailors were temporarily raised by a signal from the *Niña,* which was a short distance in advance, announcing that land was positively in sight. This also proved to be a mistake, and doubts began to be entertained as to whether, in case land should be discovered, it would wait for the fleet to come up with it, or would melt away into invisibility.

Although Columbus would not change his course at the request of the Pinzons, he now announced that he had seen several highly respectable birds flying southwest, and that he had made up his mind to follow them. This may have pleased the Pinzons, but it did not satisfy the sailors. They came aft to the sacred precincts of the quarter-deck, and informed Columbus that they were going home. Unhappy men! The Admiral instantly began a speech of tremendous length, in which he informed them that he should continue the voyage until land should be reached, no matter how long it might last. The more the men clamored, the more persistently Columbus continued his speech, and the result was that they finally went back to their quarters, exhausted and quite unable to carry out their intention of throwing him overboard.

The very next morning a branch of a thorn-bush; a board which had evidently been subjected to the influences of some sort of saw-mill, and a stick which bore the marks of a jack-knife, floated by. There could be no doubt now that land was near at last, and the mutinous sailors became cheerful once more.

It was certainly rather odd that those branches, boards, and sticks happened to come in sight just at the moment when they were needed to revive the spirits of the men, and that during the entire voyage, whenever a bird, a whale, a meteor, or other sign of land was wanted, it always promptly appeared. Columbus expresses in his journal the opinion that this was providential, and evidently thought that, on the whole, it was a handsome recognition of his transcendent merits. Concerning this we are not required to give any decision.

The wind blew freshly from the east, and the fleet sailed rapidly before it. In the evening Columbus fancied that he saw a light, which he assumed to be a lantern in the hands of some one on land. He called the attention of a sailor to it, who of course agreed with his commander that the light was a shore light. At about two o'clock on the following morning—the 12th of October—a sailor on board the *Pinta*, named Rodrigo de Triana, positively saw land—this time without any postponement.

Most of us have been taught to believe that the discovery of the New World was signalized by the joyful cry of " Land ho! from the *Pinta*." A little reflection will show the gross impossibility that this exclamation was ever made by anybody connected with the expedition. In the first place, " Land ho! from the *Pinta*" is an English sentence, and, so far as is known, neither Columbus nor any of his officers or men knew a word of English. Then the expression would have been meaningless. What was "Land ho! from the *Pinta*"? and why should the sailors have referred to vague and unintelligible land of that nature, when their thoughts were fixed on the land which lay on the near horizon? Obviously this story is purely mythical, and should no longer have a place in history.

As soon as it was certain that land was in sight, the fleet hove-to and waited for daylight. The voyage was ended at last. Columbus was about to set foot on transatlantic soil, and the sailors were full of hope that the rum of the strange land would be cheap and palatable. Perhaps the only unhappy man on board the fleet was Rodrigo de Triana, who first saw the land but did not receive the promised reward; Columbus appropriating it to himself, on the ground that, having fancied he saw a hypothetical lantern early in the evening, he was really the first to see land, and had honestly and fairly earned the reward. Let us hope that he enjoyed it, and felt proud whenever he thought of his noble achievement.

CHAPTER VII.

THE DISCOVERY.

WHEN the day dawned, an island was seen to be close at hand, and the desire to go ashore was so keen that in all probability little attention was paid to breakfast. The officers put on all their best clothes, and Columbus and the two Pinzons, each bearing flags with appropriate devices, entered the boats and were rowed ashore. What were considered appropriate devices to be borne on banners such as were used on the occasion of the landing of Columbus, we do not know, the historians having forgotten to describe the banners with minuteness. Perhaps "Heaven bless our Admiral" and "Cuba Libre" were the so-called appropriate devices.

The natives, assuming that Columbus and his companions had a brass band with them, which would begin to play when the boats should reach the shore, precipitately fled, and concealed themselves. As soon as he landed, Columbus threw himself on his knees, kissed the earth, and recited a prayer. He then took possession of the island in due form, and announced that it was called San Salvador; though how he had thus early discovered its name we are not told. Everybody was then made to take an oath of allegiance to Columbus as Viceroy, in the presence of the notary whom he had so thoughtfully brought with him.

Business being thus properly attended to, the sailors were allowed to amuse themselves by tasting the strange fruits which they saw before them, and by searching earnestly but without success for a wine-shop.

The natives gradually took courage and approached the strangers, whom they decided to be emigrants from heaven. Columbus smiled sweetly on them, and gave them beads, pocket-knives, pin-cushions, back numbers of the *Illustrated London News*, and other presents such as are popularly believed to soothe the savage breast. As, however, they did not seem to appreciate the Admiral's speeches, and as the sailors could find no rum, the order was given to return to the ships. The natives thereupon launched their canoes and paddled out to the vessels to return the visit of the Spaniards. They brought with them specimens of a novel substance now known as cotton, and a few small gold ornaments, which created much enthusiasm among the sailors. The Admiral promptly proclaimed that gold, being a royal monopoly, he only had the right to buy it, and that, in view of the immense importance which he foresaw that cotton would assume in dressmaking and other industries, he should conduct the cotton speculations of that expedition himself. As the natives, when the conversation turned upon gold, mentioned that, though there was no gold in San Salvador, the islands farther south were full of it, Columbus only waited to lay in wood and water, improving the time by a boat expedition along the coast, and then set sail in search of fresh discoveries.

During the next few days a number of small islands were discovered, all of which were flowing with copper-colored natives and wild fruit, but they did not appear to produce gold. The natives were in all cases amiable and full of respect for the supposed heavenly visitors, but they stoutly denied that they had any gold. Indeed, had they been questioned about chills and fever, instead of gold, they could not have been more unanimous in asserting that their particular island was entirely free from it, but that it abounded in the next island farther south.

All these islands belonged to the Bahama group, but Columbus assumed that they were in the neighborhood of Japan, and that the mainland of Asia must be within a few days' sail. As soon therefore as the sameness of constantly discovering new islands began to pall upon him, he set sail for Cuba, where, as the natives told him, there was a king whose commonest articles of furniture were made of gold. He thought it would be well to visit this deserving monarch, and buy a few second-hand tables and bedsteads from him, and then to sail straight to Asia; and so accomplish the real purpose of his voyage.

It is a pity that we are not told whether the natives talked Spanish, or whether Columbus spoke the copper-colored language. When so many discussions on the subject of gold were had, it is evident that somebody must have made rapid progress in learning one language or the other, and from what we know of the Admiral's conversational powers, it is quite probable that he mastered the San Salvadorian grammar and spelling-book, and was able to read, write, and speak the language within the first twenty-four hours after landing.

On the 28th of October Columbus reached Cuba, having picked up a host of small islands on the way. He was delighted with its appearance, and decided that, instead of being an island, it must be the mainland. For days he coasted along the shore, frequently landing and examining the deserted huts from which the inhabitants had fled on his approach. Judging from the entries made by Columbus in his journal, there was never such another island since the world began; but he is compelled to admit that the natives were not sociable. In fact, he never exchanged words with them until the interpreter whom he had brought from San Salvador threw himself overboard and swam ashore. The natives, regarding him as less ferocious and dangerous than a boat, permitted him to land, and listened to his account of the Spaniards. They were even induced to launch their canoes and visit the ships, where they were received by Columbus, who assured them that he had no connection with the Emperor of China—a statement which must have struck them as somewhat irrelevant and uncalled for.

The place where this interview was held is now known as Savanna la Mar. The harbor being a safe one, Columbus decided to remain and repair his ships, and to send an embassy by land to Pekin, which he was confident could not be more than two days' journey into the interior. Two Spaniards and the San Salvadorian native were selected as ambassadors, and supplied with a letter and presents for the Chinese Emperor, and Columbus with much liberality gave them six days in which to go to Pekin and return.

After they had departed, the ships were careened and caulked, and other little jobs were invented to keep the men out of mischief. As to gold, the natives told the old story. There was none of it in their neighborhood, but there was an island farther south where it was as common and cheap as dirt. Seeing how the description pleased the Admiral, they kindly threw in a tribe of natives with one eye in their forehead, and a quantity of select cannibals, and thus increased his desire to visit so remarkable an island.

In six days the ambassadors returned. They had found neither Pekin nor the

Chinese Emperor—nothing, in fact, except a small village, a naked chief, and a community of placid savages who had no gold and were entirely devoid of interest. They brought back with them a few cold potatoes, a vegetable hitherto unknown to Europeans, and they casually mentioned that they had seen natives in the act of smoking rolls of dark-colored leaves, but they attached no importance to the discovery, and regarded it as a curious evidence of pagan degradation. Little did they know that the dark-colored leaves were tobacco, and that the natives were smoking Partagas, Villar-y-Villar, Intimidads, and other priceless brands of the Vuelt Abajo. The sailors were cursing the worthlessness of a new continent which produced neither rum, wine, nor beer, and yet it was the native land of tobacco! Thus does poor fallen human nature fix its gaze on unattainable rum and Chinese Emperors, and so overlook the cigars that are within its reach.

CHAPTER VIII.

ADVENTURES ON LAND.

ON the 12th of November Columbus set sail in search of the gold- and cannibal-bearing island described by the natives and called Babeque. He took with him a few pairs of Cubans for the Madrid Zoological Garden, whom he intended to convert to Christianity in his leisure hours. Babeque was said to be situated about east-by-south from Cuba, and accordingly the fleet steered in that direction, skirting the Cuban coast. Two days later a head-wind and a heavy sea induced Columbus to put back to Cuba, where he waited for a fair wind. On the 19th he again put to sea, but was soon compelled for the second time to return.

When Martin Alonzo Pinzon, on board the *Pinta*, which was in the advance, saw the Admiral's signal of recall, he promptly and with great energy paid no attention to it. He astutely observed that as there might not be gold and cannibals enough in Babeque for the whole fleet, it would save trouble if he were to take in privately a full cargo, and thus avoid the hard feelings which might result from an attempt to divide with the crews of the other vessels. Pinzon therefore kept the *Pinta* on her course, and the next morning she was out of sight of the flag-ship. Columbus, not understanding the excellent intentions of his subordinate, was greatly vexed, and feared that Pinzon would sail back to Spain and claim the whole credit of discovering the New World. However, pursuit was out of the question, the *Pinta* being the fastest vessel of the fleet; and the Admiral therefore sailed back to Cuba, and while awaiting a change of wind renewed his exploration of the coast.

On the 5th of December, the weather having improved, Columbus started for the third time in search of Babeque. He soon sighted a large and beautiful island, at which his Cubans besought him not to land, since it was inhabited by one-eyed cannibals who made it a point to eat all visitors, either from motives of hunger or as a mark of respect. The Cubans admitted that the island contained gold as well as cannibals, but maintained that it was not Babeque, but Bohio.

Of course Columbus disregarded their advice, and, after anchoring for a night in a convenient harbor, proceeded to sail along the coast, landing from time to time. He found that it was a very respectable island, but the natives refused to have anything to do with him, and fled into the forest as soon as his boats touched the shore. One day, however, his men succeeded in capturing a young woman— with the usual amount of eyes, and fashionably dressed in a gold nose-ring— whom they carried before the Admiral. The latter, putting on a pair of thick blue goggles in the interests of propriety, spoke kindly to the young person, and gave her some clothes. It may be doubted whether the Admiral's old coats and trousers were particularly becoming to the fair prisoner; but as they were novelties in dress, she was greatly pleased with them, and agreed to accompany a party of middle-aged and discreet sailors to her father's village. Thus friendly relations were at last established with the natives, and Columbus, seeing the effect of clothing on the female mind, was so closely reminded of the women of Spain that he named the new island Hispaniola.

The absence of both gold and one-eyed cannibals convinced him that Hispaniola could not be Babeque, and on December 14th he once more set sail in search of that mythical island. He found nothing but the little island of Tortugas, and was finally compelled by head-winds to sail back to Hispaniola. He now made up his mind that Babeque was the Mrs. Harris of islands, and that in fact there was no such place. It pained him to give up all hope of seeing the one-eyed cannibals; but after all he must have perceived that, even if he had found them, they could not have been any real comfort to him, unless he could have seen them sitting down to dine off the faithless Pinzon.

On the 16th of December we find him anchored near Puerto de Paz, enjoying the society of a cacique, or native chief, who told him the old, old story of gold-bearing islands farther south, and in other ways did his best to meet the Admiral's views. Six days later, when near the Bay of Acul, the flag-ship was met by a canoe containing an envoy of the cacique Guacanagari, the most powerful of the native chiefs of that region. Guacanagari sent Columbus presents of cotton cloth, dolls, parrots of great resources in point of profanity, and other welcome articles. He invited Columbus to visit him at his palace, which invitation was accepted, and the cacique and the Admiral became warm friends. A few bits of gold were given to the Spaniards, and the usual story concerning Babeque was told; but Columbus had now pledged himself to total abstinence from Babeque in every form, and paid no attention to it.

Guacanagari's village was situated a few miles east of the Bay of Acul, and thither Columbus resolved to bring his ships. About midnight on Christmas eve Columbus went below, because, as he alleged, there was a dead calm and his presence on deck was not required. The judicial mind will, however, note the fact that it is not unusual for mariners to feel the need of sleep after the festivities of Christmas eve. Following the example of their commander, the entire crew hastened to fall asleep, with the exception of a small-boy to whom the wheel was confided by a drowsy quartermaster. A current steadily drifted the vessel toward the land, and in a short time the boy at the wheel loudly mentioned that the ship had struck. The Admiral was soon on deck —which shows that perhaps, after all, it was nothing stronger than claret punch— and in time succeeded in awakening the crew. The ship was hard and fast on a reef, and he ordered the mast to be cut away, and dispatched a boat to the *Niña* for assistance.   It soon became evident that the *Santa Maria* would go to pieces, and accordingly Columbus and all his men sought refuge on board the other vessel.

Guacanagari was full of grief at the disaster, and sent his people to assist in saving whatever of value the wreck contained. He came on board the *Niña* and invited the Spaniards to come to his village and occupy houses which he had set apart for them. Here he entertained them with games—base-ball, pedestrian matches, and such like pagan spectacles—while the Spaniards, not to be outdone in politeness, fired off a cannon, and thereby nearly frightened the natives to death. Meanwhile Columbus kept up a brisk trade, exchanging rusty nails for gold, of which latter metal the natives now produced considerable quantities. The cacique, finding that gold was the one thing which, above all others, distracted the

Admiral's mind from his unfortunate shipwreck, sent into the interior and collected so much that the Spaniards imagined that at last they had really reached the golden island of Babeque.

The sailors were delighted with the place. To be sure, there was no rum; but with that exception they had everything that the seafaring heart could desire. They spent their time lying in the shade, waited on by obsequious natives and fed with turtle-soup and roast chicken. The longer they tried this sort of life, the more they perceived the folly of going back to the forecastle and its diet of salt horse. They therefore proposed to Columbus that, instead of building a new ship, he should leave half of his men on the island as colonists. The Admiral was pleased with the plan. It would be cheaper to leave two or three dozen men behind him than to carry them back to Spain, and if he had a real colony in his newly discovered western world, it would add to his importance as Viceroy. So he announced that he had decided to colonize the island, and ordered his men to build a fort with the timbers of the wrecked flag-ship. The natives lent their aid, and in a short time a substantial fort, with a ditch, drawbridge, flag-staff, and everything necessary to the comfort of the garrison, was erected. It was mounted with two or three spare cannons, and Guacanagari was told that it was designed to defend his people from the attacks of the Caribs, a tribe which frequently made war on the peaceful islanders. The fort was then dignified with the title of "La Navidad,"—which is the Spanish way of spelling "nativity," although it does not do the Spaniards much credit,—and the flag of Castile and Aragon was hoisted on the flag-staff.

Thirty-nine men, under the command of Diego de Arana, the notary, were selected to garrison La Navidad. Among them were a tailor, a carpenter, a baker, and a shoemaker, while De Arana in his capacity of notary was of course able to draw up wills, protest bills of exchange, and take affidavits. Columbus did not venture to leave a plumber behind him, justly fearing that if he did the plumber would send in bills to the natives which would goad them into an indiscriminate massacre of the whole colony. All other necessary trades were, however, represented among the colonists, from which circumstance we gather that the Spanish marine was manned chiefly by mechanics.

Having organized his colony, Columbus determined to hasten back to Spain, lest Pinzon should reach home before him and publish an unauthorized work with some such striking title as "How I found the New World," and thereby injure the reputation of the Admiral and the sale of the only authentic account of the expedition. There were rumors that Pinzon's vessel had been seen lying at anchor on the eastern side of the island, but all efforts to find him failed. It was only too probable that he was on his way back to Spain, and it was important that he should not arrive home before his rightful commander.

Before sailing, Columbus made a farewell address to the colonists, closely modelled upon the Farewell Address of Washington. He warned them to beware of entangling alliances with the native women, and to avoid losing the affection and respect of Guacanagari and his people. The sailors promised to behave with the utmost propriety, and winked wickedly at one another behind the Admiral's back. The Spaniards then gave a grand farewell entertainment to the estimable cacique, who once more wept on the bosom of the Admiral, and finally, on the 4th of January, 1493, Columbus sailed for Spain.

CHAPTER IX.

THE HOMEWARD VOYAGE.

THE wind, as usual, was dead ahead, and the *Niña* made slow progress. For two days she lay at anchor in a quiet bay, but the Admiral was so anxious to reach Spain in advance of Pinzon that he would not wait any longer for a change of wind. Before he had succeeded in getting out of sight of land, the missing *Pinta* was sighted, and, Columbus's anxiety being partially relieved, the two ships put back and anchored at the mouth of a river. The interview between Pinzon and the Admiral must have been interesting. It is evident from many things that, since his great voyage had been successful, Columbus had ceased to be the conversational bane of humanity, and had become a reasonably taciturn man. On this occasion Pinzon found him painfully silent. That troubled mariner attempted to account for his desertion by saying it was all an accident, and that he had lain awake night after night bewailing the cruel fate which had separated him from his beloved commander. He was ready to swear all sorts of maritime oaths that he had never meant to part company and cruise alone.

The Admiral gloomily remarked that, while no man should be held accountable for an accident, he felt that it was his duty to mention that hereafter any officer found guilty of the commission of a similar accident would be court-martialled and hanged, after which Pinzon was permitted to return to his ship.

In view of the fact that Pinzon commanded the larger ship and could probably have beaten the *Niña* in a fair fight, the Admiral was wise in accepting his excuses and affecting to believe his story. He afterward learned that Pinzon had really been at anchor on the eastern side of the island, where it was reported that he had been seen, and that he had secured a large quantity of gold; but it was judged injudicious to ask him to surrender the gold to the Admiral. Thus harmony between Columbus and Pinzon was thoroughly restored, and they hated and distrusted each other with great vigor.

The meeting of the *Pinta* and the *Niña* was, we may presume, celebrated in due form, for Columbus, although he was a very abstemious man, asserts in his journal that at this time he saw several mermaids. We do not know what Pinzon saw; but if the abstemious Admiral saw mermaids, the less decorous Pinzon probably saw a sea-serpent and a procession of green monkeys with spiked Prussian helmets on their heads.

On the 9th of January the ships again weighed anchor and sailed along the coast, stopping from time to time to trade with the natives. At Samana Bay the Spaniards found a tribe of fierce savages, with whom they had a skirmish which resulted in wounding two of the enemy. Nevertheless, the local cacique made peace the next day, and told Columbus a very meritorious and picturesque lie concerning an island inhabited by a tribe of Amazons. Recent events indicate that in fighting and lying the present inhabitants of Samana Bay are no unworthy representatives of those whom Columbus met.

When, on the 16th of January, Columbus made positively his last departure for Spain, he intended to stop on the way and discover Porto Rico, which lay a little southward of his true course. To this, however, the sailors strongly objected. They had discovered as many islands as, in their opinion, any reasonable man could desire, and they pined for Palos and its rum-shops. They did not break out into mutiny, but they expressed their feelings so plainly, by singing "Home Again" and other depressing songs, that Columbus felt the wisdom of gratifying them—especially in view of the probability that Pinzon would again give him the slip at the first opportunity. The sailors were therefore ordered to square away the yards, and the ships were put before the fair west wind with their several bowsprits pointing straight toward Palos. Joy filled the bosoms and heightened the ruddy tint of the noses of the crew. That night they thought more highly of Columbus than ever before, and remarked among themselves that they were glad to see that the old man could restrain his unnatural thirst for islands when it became clearly necessary for him to do so.

It was not long before the fleet—if two vessels can be regarded as a fleet, except in the United States Navy—came into the region where the trade-winds constantly blow from the east. Columbus may not have recognized them as trade-winds, but he perfectly understood that they were head-winds, and with a view of avoiding them steered in a northerly direction. He succeeded in getting out of the region of perpetual east winds, but he reached the latitude where storms-centres moving rapidly to the east and south, together with areas of depression in the region of the lakes and rain in the New England and Middle States—in short, all the worst varieties of weather in the repertoire of the Signal Service Bureau—prevail. The pilots soon lost all idea of the course which the vessels had sailed, and as each one entertained a different opinion about the matter, while Columbus differed from them all and made it a practice to confuse their minds with opinions on navigation of the most intricate character, there was a certain lack of cordial and intelligent agreement among the navigators of the fleet.

About the middle of February a succession of tremendous tempests overtook the vessels. For days they drove before a gale which carried them in a north-easterly direction and threatened every moment to sink them and hide all vestiges of the great transatlantic expedition beneath the waves. Pinzon, owing to the injured condition of his mast, had no control over his ship, and was soon carried out of sight of Columbus. The latter felt that the time had come to employ all his knowledge of seamanship.

An ordinary prosaic ship-captain of the present day, finding himself in a like situation, would have brought his ship down to a close-reefed maintopsail, and, bringing the wind on his starboard quarter, would have steered about east by south, and so carried the ship out of the cyclone in two or three hours. Columbus, however, was far too scientific a navigator to adopt any such commonplace expedient. He mustered his crew, and ordered them to draw lots to see who should vow to make pilgrimages in case they should succeed in reaching land. He himself drew a lot which required him to make one pilgrimage to Santa Clara de Moguer, and another to Santa Maria de Guadalupe, and, in addition, to pay for a series of masses and to present candles to the Blessed Virgin.

As this manœuvre, which was at that time regarded as one of the most abstruse known to mariners, unaccountably failed to better the condition of the ship, the entire crew vowed to march to the first available church bare-footed and clad only in their shirts. The frightful nature of the storm may be imagined from the fact that, in spite of this splendid display of Spanish seamanship, the *Niña* continued to exhibit a determined propensity to go to pieces or to founder. Having thus done everything that a sailor could do, and all without avail, Columbus yielded to the promptings of superstition, and filling a quantity of empty casks with sea-water placed them in the hold, where he hoped they would render the ship somewhat stiffer. The *Niña* at once became steadier and ceased to try to lie over on her side, and it is quite possible that Columbus believed that his superstitious use of casks had more to do with the salvation of the ship than all the combined vows of the Admiral and his men.

While in imminent danger of drowning, Columbus had the cool forethought to write a full account of his discoveries. He enclosed the manuscript in a water-tight barrel, which he threw overboard after having attached to it a written request that the finder would return it to Christopher Columbus, or his representatives at Cadiz, Spain, where he would be suitably rewarded. It has not yet been found, but it is the intention of Dr. Schliemann, the discoverer of the personal jewelry of Helen of Troy, to discover it whenever he can spare a few days from more important discoveries.

On the 15th of February land was sighted. It was the island of St. Mary's, one of the Azores, but no one except Columbus had any idea that the *Niña* was farther north than the latitude of Lisbon. No sooner had the land been sighted than the wind changed to the north-east, and it was two days before the *Niña* could reach the island and anchor under its lee.

As for the *Pinta*, it was believed that in her crippled condition she must have perished in the storm, and as a matter of course Columbus felt extremely sorry that Pinzon could no longer display his insubordinate and unprincipled want of respect for his superior officer.

Of course everybody was anxious to go ashore at once. The sailors anticipated that rum could be found on the island, it being inhabited by civilized and Christian people, and Columbus, who, we may suppose, was not very well satisfied that he had been selected by lot to make two pilgrimages and spend a quantity of money in masses and candles, was anxious to see the crew parade for attendance on divine worship in their shirts. But the Azores belonged to Portugal, and though the Portuguese king had refused to assist Columbus in his plans of exploration, he was very indignant that any other monarch should have helped the Italian adventurer, and felt that Columbus had treated him disrespectfully by accepting Spanish help. Knowing all this, Columbus remained on shipboard and sent a boat ashore to inquire if there was a church near at hand.

The inhabitants of the island were greatly astonished to learn that the weather-beaten ship lying at anchor was the remnant of the exploring expedition which had sailed six months earlier from Palos. The Governor of the island, Juan de Casteneda, had been ordered by the Portuguese king to arrest Columbus, in case he should visit the Azores, for the offence of discovering continents without a license from the Portuguese. De Casteneda therefore was anxious to induce Columbus to land, but by too great zeal he overreached himself.

As soon as it was ascertained that there was a shrine on the island, Columbus ordered his men to fulfil their vow by marching in procession to it in their untrammelled shirts. One half the crew were detailed for this pious duty, and the Admiral intended to march with the other half as soon as the first division should return. The hasty Governor waited till the procession had entered the shrine, and then arrested every one of its members, on the frivolous plea of dressing in a way adapted to outrage the feelings of the public and to excite a breach of the peace. When

Columbus found his men did not return, he weighed anchor and stood in toward the shore. He was met by a boat containing the Governor, who declined to come on board the *Niña*, and conducted himself generally in such a suspicious way that Columbus lost his temper and called him unpleasant names. He held up his commission with its enormous seal, and told the Governor to look at it and comprehend that sealing-wax was not lavished in that way except upon officers of distinguished merit. The Governor not only insulted Columbus, but he spoke derisively of the sealing-wax, and then rowed back to land, resolved to keep his shirt-clad prisoners until he could add Columbus himself to the collection.

The usual gale soon after sprang up, and the *Niña* was driven out to sea and kept there in very unpleasant circumstances for several days. When at length Columbus again returned to his anchorage, De Casteneda sent two priests and a notary to inspect his papers. They found that his commission was properly made out, that the ship had a clean bill of health, and that her clearance from Guacanagari's customhouse was without a flaw. They then informed him that the Governor had been compelled to exercise a little caution lest vessels arriving from the West Indies should introduce yellow fever into the Azores, but that he was now entirely satisfied and would be glad to have Columbus call on him. The next morning he liberated the men whom he had made prisoners, and let them return to their ship and their trousers, it being evident that he could not hope to arrest Columbus, now that the latter was on his guard.

Having regained possession of his men, Columbus set sail for home on the 24th of the month. In about a week another storm, more violent than any which had preceded it, struck the unhappy voyagers. Once more the splendid seamanship of the commander was displayed by an order for all hands to draw lots for pilgrimages. This time the loser was to walk barefooted to the shrine of Santa Maria de la Cueva, and when Columbus found that he had once more drawn the losing lot, he must have made a private vow to play henceforth some other game in which he might have some little chance to win something. It is impossible to repress the suspicion that the vow afterward made by the crew to eat nothing but bread and drink nothing but water for a week, was made in accordance with the determination of the Admiral that he should not be the only person to perform painful and difficult feats of practical seamanship.

During the worst of the storm, and in the middle of the night, land was seen, and the ship had a narrow escape from being dashed upon it. When daylight appeared, it was found that the mouth of the Tagus was close at hand; and although it was obviously dangerous for Columbus to venture into Portuguese waters, he sailed into the river and anchored in a sheltered place near the rock of Cintra. He lost no time in sending letters, by the District Telegraph messengers of the period, to the Spanish and Portuguese monarchs, and asked of the latter permission to sail up the river to Lisbon. This request was obviously a hollow form. Lisbon was the last place to which the Admiral would have been willing to take his ship, but he wanted to convince the Portuguese king that he had the utmost confidence in him.

CHAPTER X.

HIS RECEPTION, AND PREPARATION FOR A SECOND EXPEDITION.

EVERYBODY who could hire a horse or a boat came from the surrounding country to see the ship that had crossed the Atlantic. The Portuguese nobly forgot the years in which Columbus had lived in Portugal and talked their fellow-countrymen into untimely graves, and they gave him as enthusiastic reception as an American town gives to a successful pedestrian. Presently there came a letter from King John of Portugal, inviting Columbus to come to his palace at Valparaiso, near Lisbon. The crew of the *Niña*, having reached a Christian country where, by the orders of the King, they were supplied with wine without limit and without price, were perfectly contented to defer returning to their families at Palos, and were, on the whole, rather anxious that their commander should leave them for a few days. Columbus, much against his will, felt compelled to accept the King's invitation, and was kindly received at Valparaiso.

Of course Columbus, when he described the results of his voyage, could not deny himself the pleasure of reminding King John that he might have had the glory of sending out the expedition. He told the King that he was really sorry for him, and hoped it would be a lesson to him never to refuse an offer made by a meritorious Genoese to find new continents for him. King John expressed his pleasure at the success of Columbus, but incidentally remarked that he presumed his seafaring friend was aware that, by the provisions of an ancient treaty and a papal bull, all the countries that Columbus had discovered undoubtedly belonged to Portugal.

This conversation was not altogether satisfactory to Columbus, but he would have been still more dissatisfied had he known the advice which the King's councillors gave him. They said there was not the least doubt that the native Indians on board the *Niña* had been stolen from the Portuguese East Indies, and that Columbus ought to be immediately killed. The King did not favor the death of Columbus, but suggested that the truly honorable course to pursue would be to dismiss Columbus in the respectful manner due to his gallant conduct, and to send immediately a secret expedition to take possession of the countries which he had discovered. In accordance with this decision, Columbus was treated with great politeness, and returned to his ship, quite ignorant of his narrow escape from death, and in excellent spirits with the exception of a slight uneasiness as to the amount of truth that might exist in the King's remark about ancient treaties and papal balls. Sailing from the Tagus, he reached Palos in two days, and landed on the 15th of March.

The return of Columbus created immense surprise, and with the exception of the wives of his sailors, who, having assumed that their husbands never would return, had married again, everybody received him with enthusiasm. The shops were closed, all the boys in the schools were given a half-holiday, and the entire population flocked to the church whither Columbus and his men betook themselves as soon as they landed, to return thanks for their preservation. Columbus was no longer, in public estimation, the tedious foreigner who ought to be sent out of the country at any cost; he was one of the most remarkable men in Spain, who deserved all sorts of honors. There were any number of men who now recollected that they had always said he was a great man and would certainly discover a first-class continent, and there were very few persons in all Palos who were not confident that the encouragement which they had given to Columbus had been one of the chief causes of his success.

The King and Queen were at Barcelona, but the Admiral, having had all the sea-voyaging that his system seemed to require, decided to go to Barcelona by land instead of by water, and after writing to the monarchs, announcing his arrival, he set out for Seville, to wait for orders.

The same day on which Columbus landed, and about twelve hours later, the *Pinta* arrived. Pinzon had been driven by the storm which separated him from the *Niña* into Bayonne. Making up his mind that Columbus was safely drowned, he wrote to Ferdinand and Isabella, announcing that he had made remarkably valuable discoveries ; that he would hasten to Spain to report to them in person ; and that he was sorry to say that Columbus had found a watery grave. When he entered the harbor of Palos, and saw the *Niña* at anchor, he felt that life was a hollow mockery. He went quietly to his own house, and wrote to the monarchs a letter which, we may assume, differed somewhat in its tone from the one he had written from Bayonne. The reply was extremely cold, and forbade Pinzon to present himself at court.

The people of Palos, having already celebrated, to the utmost of their power, the arrival of Columbus, were rather annoyed at Pinzon's appearance, and thought that on the whole it was an unwarrantable liberty. That Pinzon was a really intelligent man is proved by the fact that he hastened to die a few days after he had received the monarch's unpleasant letter. There was obviously nothing else left for him to do, and he deserves credit for thus clearly perceiving his duty.

Columbus, soon after his arrival at Seville, received a flattering letter from Ferdinand and Isabella, who thanked him for his services, invited him to come to court, and mentioned that the sooner he could fit out a new expedition the better it would be. Accompanied by six Indians and a quantity of parrots, together with a collection of stuffed animals and specimens of novel trees and late West Indian designs in minerals, the Admiral proceeded to Barcelona, exciting immense enthusiasm at every town on the road, and being mistaken by the youth of Spain for some new kind of circus. On his arrival at court, the monarchs received him in great state, and asked him to take a chair and make himself at home; this being the first time within the memory of man that they had ever asked any one to be seated.

As has been said, Columbus had greatly improved in point of reticence after his discovery of the New World, but on this occasion he appears to have relapsed into his old habits. At any rate, the lecture which he proceeded to deliver was of such appalling length that when it was finished the King and Queen both fell on their respective knees in thankful prayer, and afterward ordered the *Te Deum* to be sung.

There was a slight portion of truth in the remarks made by King John of Portugal to Columbus concerning a papal bull assigning certain countries to the Portuguese Crown. It was conceded by all Christian nations of that period that the Pope owned in fee simple all the heathen countries wheresoever situated. One of the Popes had assigned to the Portuguese all those certain heathen lands situate, lying, and being in the continent of Africa, together with all and singular the heathen and other objects thereunto belonging or in any wise appertaining. This was the bull to which King John referred. It is true that it did not give him any right to lands and heathen in America, but the Spanish monarchs thought it would be wise to obtain a bull formally assigning America to them. They therefore wrote to Pope Alexander VI., informing him that they had discovered a new continent full of desirable heathen admirably fitted for conversion, and requesting a formal grant thereof. At the same time, Columbus, in order to prove the pious character of his expedition, ordered his six best Indians to be baptized.

The Pope issued the desired bull, and, in order to avoid any objection on the part of the Portuguese, divided the Atlantic by a meridian one hundred miles west of the Azores, giving to the Portuguese all the heathen lands which they might discover east of this meridian, and to the Spaniards all that they might discover west of it. This was very handsome on the part of the Pope, and showed that he was liberal and open-handed.

The news of the return of Columbus filled every European monarch with the conviction that the discovery of new continents was the only proper occupation for a monarch of spirit, and with the determination to make discoveries first and to call on the lawyers to find flaws in the Pope's bull afterward. It was therefore important that there should be no delay in sending out a second Spanish expedition. Orders were issued by the monarchs of Castile and Aragon, authorizing Columbus to buy, hire, or seize any vessels that he might find in the ports of Andalusia that were suited for exploring purposes, and to impress any officers or sailors that might suit his fancy. For ships, provisions, stores, and men thus seized fair prices were to be paid, and money was raised for this purpose from all available sources, though no man seems to have thought of the expedient of printing paper-money, and thus creating out of nothing currency enough to defray the cost of a voyage to America, and to move the West India gold and slave crops.

To assist Columbus and to conduct the business of exploration and colonization, Archdeacon Juan Rodriguez de Fonseca was made a sort of Secretary of Exploration and Superintendent of Indian Affairs, and was given very extensive powers. It may seem to us strange that a priest should have received this appointment, but priests were as numerous in Spain as Colonels now are in South Carolina, and probably all the men who were not priests were either in jail or had volunteered to join Columbus as sailors and gold-hunters. It was this able Archdeacon who chiefly organized the second expedition of Columbus, and he engaged twelve active priests well acquainted with the screw, the pulley, the wheel, and the other theologico-mechanical powers, and commanded by the Apostolic Vicar Rev. Bernardo Boyle, to convert the heathen as fast as they should be discovered.

It would violate all precedent if the story of Columbus and the egg were to be spared the readers of this volume. It is briefly as follows: Soon after his return to Spain he dined with Cardinal de Mendoza, an eminent clergyman with a talent for dinner. An objectionable young man who was present, and who undoubtedly had taken more champagne than was good for his fellow-diners, asked the Admiral if he did not think that if he had not discovered the New World some one else would very shortly have discovered it. He was unquestionably an impertinent young man, but he was undoubtedly right in assuming that sooner or later the Atlantic would have been crossed, even if Columbus had never been born. Historians tell us that Columbus, in reply, asked the young man if he could stand an egg on its little end; and when the young man, after rudely inquiring what Columbus was giving him, was constrained to admit that he could not perform the feat in question, the great explorer simply flattened the little end of the egg by knocking it against the table, and then easily made it stand upright. The whole company instantly burst into tears, and exclaimed that Columbus was the greatest and noblest of mankind.

If this trick of flattening an egg was really regarded as a brilliant repartee, by which the impertinent young man ought to have been utterly withered up, it gives us a melancholy view of the state of the art of repartee among the Spaniards. The real facts of the case are probably these: Cardinal De Mendoza, the dinner, and the impertinent young man doubtless existed in the form and manner specified; and the impertinent young man, in an advanced state of champagne, probably said something insulting to the Admiral. The latter, disdaining to notice the affront by words, and reluctant to cause any unpleasant scene at the Cardinal's dinner-table, merely threw an egg at the offender's head, and pursued his conversation with his host. Subsequent writers, determined to give a profoundly scientific character to everything the Admiral did, built up from this slight basis of fact the egg-balancing story. In point of fact, any one can balance an egg on its little end by the exercise of little care and patience, and it is rather more easy to do this with an egg that has not been flattened than with one that has.

There is another contemporaneous story which is far more credible, and requires no explanation. While Columbus was enjoying the honors which were everywhere lavished upon him, and was on visiting terms with the King and Queen, and dining with Cardinals and Aldermen and Chambers of Commerce, the unhappy sailor who first saw land, but whose promised reward was appropriated by Columbus, went to Africa and turned Mahometan, in disgust at his treatment. Probably Columbus thought that, in the circumstances, this was a delicate and considerate act, for the sight of the man could hardly have given much satisfaction to the Admiral who had pocketed the reward.

Meanwhile King John of Portugal was busy fitting out an expedition ostensibly to explore the coast of Africa, but really to discover transatlantic countries. He tried to induce the Pope to give him the islands discovered by Columbus, and informed Ferdinand and Isabella that he was advised by his counsel that, under the authority of the early bull already referred to, any countries that might be discovered south of a line drawn westward from the Canaries were, in the eye of the law, a part of Africa, and as such would belong to Portugal. The Spanish monarchs conducted the diplomatic dispute with him in the ablest manner, sending to Portugal their most tedious ambassadors, and thus prolonging the negotiations as long as possible.

Columbus, refusing all offers to lecture

before the Spanish lyceums, hurried forward his own expedition so as to sail before the Portuguese fleet could be made ready. With the aid of Fonseca and the latter's two chief assistants, Francisco Pinelo and Juan de Soria, he collected seventeen ships, their crews, and a large company of colonists, and all the supplies and live-stock needed for planting an imposing colony. There was no lack of volunteers. Every man who thirsted for adventure, and every ruined nobleman who wanted to repair his broken fortunes, was eager to accompany Columbus; and even the small-boys, excited by a desire to scalp Indians, were anxious to run away and ship as cabin-boys on board the fleet. No less than fifteen hundred persons were either accepted as volunteers or accompanied the expedition as stowaways, and among them was as fine and varied a collection of scoundrels as had ever set sail from an alleged Christian country.

The expedition was not organized without several disputes between Columbus and Fonseca. The latter complained that the Admiral wanted too many servants, including footmen, coachmen, and other gaudy and useless followers; while the Admiral, in his turn, insisted that the Archdeacon could not be made to understand that footmen were absolutely necessary to the work of exploration. The King, when appealed to, always decided that Columbus was right; but it is doubtful if Fonseca's affection for the Admiral was thereby greatly increased. Finally all was ready, and on the 25th of September, 1493, the second personally conducted transatlantic expedition of Christopher Columbus set sail from Cadiz.

CHAPTER XI.

EXPLORATIONS IN THE WEST INDIES.

THE voyage was smooth and prosperous. The expedition reached the Canaries on the 1st of October, where Columbus laid in a supply of chickens, sheep, goats, calves, and pigs. It is interesting to know that these were the pioneer pigs of America. They were eight in number, and from them descended most of the pigs that now inhabit the West India islands. On October 7th the fleet again weighed anchor, and by order of its Admiral steered in a rather roundabout direction for the islands which were supposed to lie south of Hispaniola. Columbus was determined—of course for the noblest and most public-spirited reasons— that no one but himself should know the true route to the New World; but his trick of steering first in one direction and then in another could not have had the desired effect of puzzling any really intelligent sailor. This time whales, floating bushes, and other signs of land were not needed to cheer the crews, and consequently they were not seen—a circumstance that strengthens in the minds of some persons the belief that Columbus on his first voyage secretly dropped these signs of land overboard from the bow of his vessel, and then called his men to look at them. In the latter part of the voyage a heavy thunder-storm occurred, and while it was in progress lights were seen at the tops of the masts and elsewhere aloft. These electrical phenomena, called by the sailors "St. Elmo's candles," were received with much satisfaction as evident tokens that the saint was busily taking care of the vessels. As he is an able and careful saint, it is perhaps impertinent to criticise his methods, but it does seem rather odd that he cannot take care of a ship without running the risk of setting her on fire by the reckless use of naked and unprotected lights. This was the only storm of consequence that was met on the passage, and, thanks to St. Elmo! it does not seem to have done any harm.

On the 3d of November, which was Sunday, the island of Dominica was sighted, and the usual hymns were sung and prayers were said. So many islands soon came in sight that it was difficult to select one on which to land. In this embarrassment of riches, the Admiral finally landed on an island which he called Marigalante, after the name of the flag-ship. It was a fair average sort of island, but after taking formal possession of it and of all other islands, visible and invisible, belonging to the same group, Columbus left it and sailed to the island of Guadalupe, a few miles distant, where he landed on November 4th.

There was a village near the shore, but the inhabitants fled as the Spaniards landed, leaving behind them only a few useless babies. Searching the houses, Columbus discovered the stern-post of a

European vessel, which must have drifted across the Atlantic, since it was much too large to have been sent through the Post Office, even if we assume—which is grossly improbable—that any native had written to Europe and ordered a stern-post. From the number of human bones which were found in the ash-barrels and garbage-boxes at this village, it was suspected that the people were cannibals, as in fact they were, being no other than the fierce and cruel Caribs.

Pursuing his voyage along the coast, Columbus again landed and explored more deserted villages, capturing a woman and a boy who had lingered a little too long behind the absconding villagers. On returning to his ship, the Admiral was pained to learn that one of his officers, Captain Diego Marque, and eight men, who had gone ashore without orders, had not yet returned, and were probably already undergoing preparation for a Caribbean dinner. Alonzo de Ojeda, a young nobleman who afterward became famous as one of the ablest and most cruel of Spanish explorers, was sent on shore in command of a detachment to search for the missing men, and to bring back as much of them as might remain uneaten. Ojeda searched in vain, and returned with the report that Marque and his comrades could not be found, even in the unsatisfactory shape of cold victuals. Several women who came on board the fleet, announcing that they were runaway slaves, told frightful stories of the atrocities perpetrated by the Caribs, and the missing men were universally believed to have been killed and eaten. At last, after several days, Marque and his men appeared on the shore, extremely ragged and hungry. They had merely lost themselves in the woods, and had not seen a single cannibal. Of course some indignation was felt at this trivial end of what had been mistaken for a terrible tragedy, and Columbus promptly punished the delinquents, ostensibly for being absent without leave.

On the 14th of November, after sailing

hither and thither through the Caribbean archipelago, the fleet anchored at the island of Santa Cruz. The natives fled into the interior as usual, but a canoe-load of Indians made its appearance a little later, and, on being chased by one of the Spanish boats, shot showers of poisoned arrows at the pursuers. After a lively battle, in which a Spaniard was fatally wounded and one of the Indians was killed, the canoe was sunk and the survivors captured. They were so fierce and ugly in appearance that they were instantly judged to be cannibals of the deepest dye, and were loaded with chains and afterward sent to Spain as curiosities.

So many new islands were now sighted that Columbus, whose stock of names was growing small, called one of them St. Ursula, and the others her eleven thousand virgins. It is true that there were not eleven thousand islands; but as St. Ursula never had eleven thousand virgins, the name was not so extremely inappropriate. The exact number of these islands was finally ascertained to be fifty.

Discovering Porto Rico, and devoting two days to exploring its coast-line, Columbus steered for Hispaniola, which he reached on the 22d of November. The natives came off to the fleet in boats, and were remarkably polite; but Columbus did not land until he reached Samana Bay. Here he sent one of his converted Indians on shore, dressed in the best Spanish fashion, with instructions to lecture to the natives on the grandeur of Spain; but whether the lecturer was tedious and met a deserved death at the hands of his first audience, or whether he seized the opportunity to return to the comforts of naked paganism, was never known. In any case, he never returned, and it is greatly to be feared that in his case the trouble and expense of conversion were wasted.

On the 25th the expedition anchored in a harbor to which the Admiral gave the name of Monte Christo, in honor of M.

Alexandre Dumas. On landing, the Spaniards were shocked to find four bodies, one of which was recognized by its beard as the body of a Spaniard. The circumstances in which these bodies were found showed that they had been the victims of violence, and it was at once feared that the colony of La Navidad had met with a disaster. The natives said they knew nothing about the bodies, and were so innocent in their demeanor that no one cared to suspect them of murder. The Admiral, in an anxious frame of mind, made haste to arrive at La Navidad, which he reached on the 27th, but at too late an hour to venture to land. Guns were fired and Coston night-signals burned on board the fleet, but there was no sign of life from the fort. That night a suspicion dawned upon the minds of some of the fifteen hundred adventurers that the New World was not worth finding, and that colonization was a delusion and a snare.

Before morning a canoe containing a cousin of Guacanagari came out to the fleet in search of Columbus, bringing for him some valuable presents. The visitors reported that Caribs had invaded the island, and that Guacanagari had been wounded in battle with them, and was at a distant village under the care of a doctor,—whose certificate to that effect, however, he failed to produce. As to the colony of La Navidad, he did not seem to know very much about it. He said it was his impression that the colonists had been sick; he believed some of them had moved away; and he had a vague idea that they had fought a little among themselves. Having thus cheered up the Admiral, the friendly native returned to the shore, and the Spaniards waited anxiously for daylight.

When the day finally dawned, and the Spaniards prepared to land, they were surprised to find that not a native was visible. On landing, they were still more surprised to find that the colonists had totally disappeared, that the fort was in ruins, and that Guacanagari's village was a heap of ashes. From the appearance of the fort, it was evident that it had been captured and sacked. Further search resulted in the discovery of the buried bodies of eleven Spaniards, while in the native houses farther in the interior, from which the inhabitants hastily fled, were found articles which had formerly been the property of the missing colonists.

Gradually the natives overcame their fears, and came to meet Columbus. They told a story which was intrinsically probable, and doubtless true. The colonists had conducted themselves as sailors left to themselves in a tropical climate, among gentle savages, might have been expected to. They refused to work, they adopted polygamy as their chief occupation, and, not content with quarrelling among themselves, they insulted and outraged the natives until the latter began to feel seriously provoked. After a time the two lieutenants of Don Diego de Arana, the Governor, headed a rebellion against him, but, being defeated, marched off with nine men and a large supply of wives to search for gold in the interior. Reaching the dominions of the cacique Caonabo, a powerful chief of Carib birth, they were pleasantly welcomed and cheerfully put to death. Being of the opinion that there were still more Spaniards on the island than were really needed, Caonabo formed an alliance with another chief of like views, and, falling upon the fort at night, captured it and massacred every colonist with the exception of a few who saved themselves by rushing into the sea and drowning in privacy. The friendly natives further said that they fought under the leadership of Guacanagari on the side of the Spaniards, and were badly beaten.

A coasting expedition having discovered the village where Guacanagari was residing, Columbus went to see him. He found the cacique lying in bed, surrounded by seven wives and suffering greatly. Guacanagari repeated the story of the capture of the fort, and put in evidence his wounded leg, marked "Exhibit A," as proof of the truth of his story. Unfortunately, no wound was visible, and although the cacique insisted that his leg had been utterly ruined by a heavy stone which had struck it, the Spanish surgeon was of opinion that nothing was the matter. Father Boyle, who was a most zealous ecclesiastic, held that this was an excellent opportunity for showing the islanders the merits of the Christian religion, and recommended that Guacanagari should be promptly burned at the stake. But the Admiral, although he admitted that it was difficult to explain the cacique's leg in a satisfactory way, argued that he would be much more useful raw than he would if roasted, and to prove this assertion exchanged a large quantity of glass beads with the cacique for merely their weight in gold. This demonstration satisfied the Spaniards temporarily, with the exception of Father Boyle, who was pained to find Columbus apparently subordinating Christian duty to a love of gain.

Guacanagari went on board the flagship with the Admiral, where he was much pleased with the horses, which he saw for the first time, and pronounced to be very able and ingenious animals. He was also observed to take altogether too much interest in ten women whom Columbus had carried off from the Caribbean islands. The conversation between Guacanagari and the Spaniards is said to have been constrained and awkward, as indeed it doubtless was, for no one could converse easily and pleasantly with a cacique who was constantly gazing in admiration at ten different women. Columbus, as a token of good-will, hung an image of the Virgin around Guacanagari's neck, who, when he learned that the Christians worshipped it, said he would rather not wear it, lest he should become a Christian and covet his neighbor's wife and break his neighbor's skull, like the late Christian colonists. Father Boyle was more anxious to burn him than ever after hearing this blasphemous remark; but Columbus very properly said it was inhospitable and unjustifiable to burn visitors, except in the case of a surprise-party, and that the cacique should go on shore safely, which he shortly did.

The next day Guacanagari did not return to the ship, but in his place sent his brother, who paid a great deal of attention to the Carib women, talking with them— as he said—on scientific matters. That night the ten Carib women jumped overboard and swam ashore, and when the Spaniards landed in the morning to search for them, no trace could be found either of the women or of Guacanagari. It was too evident that the cacique had fallen in love ten deep, and had eloped with his ten heart's idols. The Spaniards, who of course took no interest in the women, were shocked at the painful example of immorality set by Guacanagari, and agreed that they were now convinced that he and his hypocritical savages had either betrayed the colonists to Caonabo, or had slaughtered them and then invented Caonabo and laid the blame upon him.

CHAPTER XII.

ATTEMPTS AT COLONIZATION.

GUACANAGARI, in his last interview with Columbus, had advised him not to plant a new colony at La Navidad. He said that, while he was extremely anxious to have the Spaniards as neighbors, duty compelled him to admit that the locality was an unhealthy one, and that foreigners settling there were sure to contract chills and fever. Columbus shared the opinion that it was an unhealthy place, but he thought that colonists would be more apt to contract bloodthirsty native chiefs than peaceful malarious fever. At any rate, he was clear that it would be unwise to repeat the experiment of colonization at a place with such unpleasant associations.

Expeditions were sent along the coast to find a new location, but as no eligible building spots were found, the fleet set sail for Monte Christo. About thirty miles east of Monte Christo a fine harbor was found, and, on landing, the Admiral was so pleased with the place that he resolved to build a city without further delay. The ships were unloaded, and the animals were set on shore. A nice city, called the city of Isabella, was then laid out, with a church, a government-house, a town-pump, a custom-house, a jail, and everything that could make the colonists feel comfortable and at home.

This done, the Spaniards, including Columbus, fell sick with great unanimity. Most of them felt that they could have been sick to more advantage in Spain, and that, on the whole, they wanted their money back. If exploration consisted in crossing an inexcusably wide ocean merely to build houses among unsociable savages, and to contract marsh-fever, they were confident that they had had quite enough of it. Columbus knew that he must soon send the fleet back to Spain for fresh supplies of food, medicine, and clothing; but he disliked to send home the unsatisfactory report that the first set of colonists were all dead, and the second all sick. He therefore ordered Ojeda to get together a few comparatively well men, and to march into the interior and discover something that could be mentioned to advantage in his official report.

With a small force Ojeda marched across the mountain range that lay back of Isabella, and descended into a delightful plain, where every prospect pleased him, and the natives were less than usually vile. Gold was found to be really plentiful, and when Ojeda returned Columbus saw his way clear to writing a brilliant report, and the colonists' spirits revived.

Twelve of the ships were immediately got ready for sea and loaded with specimens of plants for the Agricultural Bureau, gold for the Spanish monarchs, and Caribs for the church. Columbus, in his report, passed lightly and skilfully over the unpleasant features of the expedition, and dwelt eloquently upon the beauty of the island, the healthful situation of the city, and the enormous wealth of the gold-mines. He also forcibly pointed out the great need which the cannibal Caribs had of being promptly converted. He proposed that Spain should send out ships laden with supplies, which he would pay for with Carib slaves, and that when the slaves reached Spain they could be converted at little expense, and made to do a great deal of work. Thus the cause of missions could be carried on at a profit of at least a hundred per cent and a joint stock company for the enslavement and conversion of Caribs would be able to declare large and frequent dividends.

Columbus had always maintained that his chief object in discovering America was to spread the Gospel, and this proposal to enslave the Caribs shows that he was sincere. Nevertheless, Queen Isabella said it would be a shame to make the poor Caribs slaves, and that she was surprised that Columbus should think of such a thing. Thus the Admiral's great missionary scheme proved abortive, but his arguments were afterward used with great success in defence of the slave-trade which stocked the Georgian and South Carolinian plantations.

On the 2d of February, 1494, the twelve ships set sail for Spain, and Columbus felt that unless the officers should prove indiscreet and tell unpleasant truths, his report would be accepted as a proof of the success of his second great expedition.

The colonists' spirits had been raised by the sight of the gold brought back by Ojeda, but they fell to a very low ebb when the ships departed. The prospect of remaining behind to die of fever, while their more fortunate companions could go home and tell magnificent stories with no one to contradict them, was very depressing. In vain did Father Boyle celebrate the very highest kind of mass in the church, and in vain did Columbus put the jail in the best possible order. Nothing could make the colonists feel contented and happy.

In these circumstances, they naturally abused the Admiral. They said he was only an Italian, any way, and had no right to command Spanish gentlemen. They even went so far as to make personal and disparaging remarks concerning organ-grinders, and expressed the opinion that an organ-grinder should stick to his monkey and refrain from meddling with exploration. There was an alleged scientific person among them—one Fermin Cedo—who pretended there were no gold-mines on the island. He said he had analyzed the gold brought back by Ojeda, and it was grossly adulterated. He admitted that the Indians did have a little real gold, but maintained that they had inherited it from their ancestors and could not find any more even if they were to try. The malcontents, under the leadership of Bernal Diaz, the comptroller, who appears to have had all the obstinacy and wrong-headedness that pertain to that office in our own day, resolved to seize the remaining ships and return to Spain, leaving Columbus to enjoy the fever by himself. Columbus, however, discovered the plot and immediately recovered his health sufficiently to arrest Diaz, to punish the least respectable of his followers, and thus to suppress the mutiny.

In order to divert his men from thoughts of fever and mutiny, the Admiral now prepared to lead an expedition into the interior. He appointed his brother Diego Governor of Isabella during his absence, and with four hundred men—all, in fact, who were well enough to march—he set out for the gold-bearing mountains of Cibao. Following the route taken by Ojeda the party crossed the nearest range of mountains, and entered the fertile plain previously mentioned. The natives were at first greatly frightened by the horsemen; and when they discovered that a horse and his rider were not made in one piece, but could be taken apart, they were more than ever filled with admiration at the mechanical ingenuity of the Spaniards.

Crossing the plain, Columbus penetrated into the mountainous region of Cibao, over which the Carib chief Caonabo ruled. Nothing, however, was seen of him, and the natives were as friendly as those of the plain. They brought gold-dust and small nuggets to Columbus, and assured him that at the distance of about a day's march gold could be found in nuggets of the size of a piece of chalk.

This originally meritorious story had now become so old that Columbus paid no attention to it, knowing that if he were to march all the rest of his life, the richest gold-mines would always be a little farther off. So he selected a convenient mountain, where he built a fort, calling it St. Thomas, which he garrisoned with fifty-six men commanded by Pedro Margarite. There appears not to have been any reason for building and garrisoning this fort, unless it was a desire on the part of the Admiral to station Margarite and his men where they could not take part in any future mutiny in Isabella.

Returning with the rest of the force, Columbus reached Isabella on the 29th of March, stopping by the way to trade with the natives and to learn their method of living. He found the people whom he had left at Isabella in a more gloomy state than ever. Their stock of medicines was nearly exhausted, and their provisions were growing scarce. He was compelled to put them on half rations, and to build a mill for grinding corn. The mill was a happy thought; but when it was built, the colonists unanimously agreed that Spanish gentlemen could not grind corn without losing their self-respect. Columbus said he rather thought they could, and he compelled every man to take his turn at grinding, thereby confirming them in the opinion that no Italian accustomed to grind out "Annie Laurie" and "Baby Mine" could possibly understand the feelings of a gentleman.

A messenger soon arrived from Fort St. Thomas, announcing that Caonabo was about to attack it. Ojeda was therefore put in command of three hundred and ninety-six men, and ordered to capture Caonabo and inaugurate the new jail with him. Ojeda, promptly started, and on his way met a Spaniard who had been robbed. Being a just man, Ojeda thereupon seized the cacique of the province, his son, and nephew, and sent them to Isabella, where Columbus, filled with horror at the crime which they had not committed, sentenced them to death—a sentence which he afterward revoked in order to show his clemency.

As nearly all the able-bodied colonists were now in the interior, Columbus thought it would be safe to undertake a small exploring voyage, and so, leaving Don Diego in charge of the city, he took three of the ships and sailed for Cuba. Had he been a selfish and heartless man, he might have imagined that during his absence the sick at Isabella would die, and the Spaniards in the interior would either starve to death or be killed by Caonabo—thus ridding him of much care and vexation. As he was not this kind of man, we can only wonder at his simplicity in dividing his forces in the face of a cruel enemy, and then calmly sailing away with the most useful of the ships. He left reams of written instructions to Margarite, Ojeda and Don Diego, pointing out to them the wickedness of quarrelling, and recommending them not to allow Caonabo to exterminate them. He also left Father Boyle behind him, probably because that zealous ecclesiastic's longing to burn somebody made him an unsafe person to take to sea, where the utmost caution in regard to fire is necessary.

CHAPTER XIII.

SEARCH FOR CHINA.—SUBJUGATION OF HISPANIOLA.

ON the 24th of April Columbus set sail, determined this time to reach the Empire of China. He anchored for a night at La Navidad, but saw nothing of Guacanagari. Sailing thence, he reached Cuba and began to coast along the south side of the island. The natives ran away as usual, and were afterward coaxed back with beads. They told him, with some variations, the familiar story of a gold-bearing island farther south, and Columbus decided to give them one more chance to prove its truth. He steered south in search of the mythical Babeque, and when he came within sight of a fine large island, he began to hope that Babeque was found at last; but it proved to be only Jamaica. Instead of running away, the natives came out in canoes to welcome the Spaniards with bloody lances to hospitable drowning-places. Without stopping to fight the first batch of seventy canoes, the fleet sailed on in search of a good harbor. When an apparently eligible place for anchoring was found, a boat was sent to make soundings, and was attacked by the natives, who swarmed on the beach. A force was therefore landed to convince the natives that their conduct was impolite; and after many of them had been shot and the rest driven into the woods in terror, with a savage dog in hot pursuit, they were convinced of their error. The local cacique sent envoys and negotiated a treaty, after which the Spaniards were permitted to repair their vessels and take in water in peace. Columbus explored the coast for some little distance to the westward, but finding no signs of gold, or of the rum for which it afterward became famous, returned to Cuba and resumed his search for China.

Day after day he sailed slowly westward,

keeping near the coast and frequently landing to inquire if China was close at hand. Sometimes the information he received gave him great encouragement. For example, one able and imaginative cacique told him of a tribe of men with tails. As it was notorious that men with tails inhabited a part of Asia, Columbus naturally thought the cacique's story referred to them, and that he would soon reach the region described by the veracious Sir John Mandeville. Another cacique told him of a king who habitually wore a white garment and was called a saint. This king Columbus immediately identified with Prester John, though he ought to have remembered that no true Presbyterian would dream of wearing white robes except in the seclusion of his bedchamber. Encouraged by these stories, the hopeful explorer sailed on toward China, now narrowly escaping shipwreck in the maze of small islands known to us as the "Keys," and now learning with astonishment what violent thunder-storms the West Indies can produce when they are needed. At one time the sea became the color of milk, which greatly alarmed the sailors. They said that putting milk into the sea was a defiance of the laws of nature, which provide that water should always be put into milk, and that they did not like to cruise in latitudes where so unnatural a practice was followed. Still, Columbus persevered. Cuba seemed really to have no end, or to be, in other words, a continent.

Finally, at the end of fifty days, when not a particle of China had been found, and the vessels were so strained as to be entirely unseaworthy, the sailors informed Columbus that this thing had gone quite far enough, and that it was time to turn back. The Admiral was so sure that Pekin must be within a few days' sail that he was very anxious to pursue the voyage, but he finally agreed to compromise the matter. He said he would turn back, provided every officer, sailor, and boy would make an affidavit that Cuba was a part of the mainland of Asia. This they consented to do with much alacrity, and when every affidavit had been duly sworn in the presence of a notary, Columbus announced that any person who should at any time express the view that Cuba was an island would be judged guilty of perjury and punished by a fine of ten thousand maravedies, or by a hundred lashes and the amputation of the tongue.

Having thus conclusively ascertained that Cuba was Asia, he steered south-east, and on the 13th of June anchored at the Isle of Pines. Had he only kept on his voyage westward a day or two longer, he would have reached the western extremity of Cuba, and would have learned that it was an island.

The voyage back along the Cuban coast was laborious, the weather being often boisterous and the winds adverse. The sailors became so worn out that Columbus was compelled to anchor in a convenient harbor and live on shore with his men for more than a week, in order that they might rest. Here he met with a venerable cacique, who gave him excellent advice as to his future conduct, and assured him that if he did not treat the natives justly he would be punished in a future world. Judging from the report of the cacique's sermon, he was almost as good a Christian as Father Boyle.

When his men were sufficiently repaired, Columbus sailed to Jamaica and resumed the exploration of its coast-line. He circumnavigated the island without meeting with any hostile demonstrations from the natives, and, although he saw no gold, he was kind enough to speak well of Jamaica in his official report. He was rather embarrassed by a particularly gorgeous cacique, arrayed in a cotton helmet and a necklace of green stones, who with his entire family boarded the flag-ship and informed the Admiral that he intended to go to Spain with him. Columbus had some difficulty in declining the cacique's company, but he finally convinced him that if he wished to take passage he must apply at the office of the company and provide himself with tickets in the usual way. The truth is, the female part of the cacique's family was numerous and beautiful, and the judicious Admiral feared that the presence of the ladies would seriously interfere with the duties of his officers.

On the 20th of August the fleet reached Hispaniola, but Columbus did not recognize it, and fancied that he had discovered a new island. A day or two later a cacique came off to meet him in a canoe, and, addressing him in broken Spanish, informed him of his true locality. Columbus therefore landed nine of his men, with orders to proceed to Isabella and report to Don Diego, and then continued his voyage along the south coast of the island. The winds, however, persistently opposed him, and he was compelled to lie at anchor for many days. This slow progress, added to the toils and cares which he had lately experienced, told heavily on the Admiral's health, already enfeebled by his illness at Isabella. He kept on his feet till the last moment, but on the 24th of September was struck down by an an attack which rendered him totally insensible, and in that condition he remained for several days, while the fleet pursued its way and finally reached Isabella.

One of the first to welcome the Admiral when he landed was his brother Bartholomew. Years before, when Columbus was seeking some monarch who would take an interest in exploration, he sent Bartholomew to England to see if King Henry VII. was that kind of king. Either the Post Office of the period was badly managed, or Christopher Columbus was so much occupied with thoughts of exploration that he forgot the existence of Bartholomew. At any rate, neither brother appears to have heard a word from the other until Bartholomew accidentally learned that the Admiral had actually discovered the New World and was on the point of fitting out a second expedition. Bartholomew had at last induced King Henry to agree to give his brother the command of an exploring expedition, but of course the news from Spain rendered this agreement useless. Bartholomew hastened to Spain by the most rapid route, and when he found on arriving that his brother had already sailed, he called on Ferdinand and Isabella, who immediately gave him three ships and sent him with supplies to the new colony.

There is no doubt that Bartholomew Columbus was an able man, to whom full justice has never been done. He was sent to England on an errand, and he stayed till it was accomplished, although it took him ten years to do it. Where is the man of the present day who would execute the wishes of a brother with this strict and patient fidelity, especially if during the whole time he should never receive a letter or a telegram from home? That Bartholomew was a bold and skilful sailor is proved by the fact that he found his way across the Atlantic to Isabella without any sailing directions, and in spite of the care that Christopher had taken to conceal the knowledge of the direct route. Evidently Bartholomew could both obey and command, and there is no reason to suppose that he was in any way inferior to his more famous brother.

The Admiral appears to have recalled without much difficulty the fact that he had once had a brother Bartholomew, and to have readily recognized him. Probably he explained that, owing to a pressure of business, Bartholomew had escaped his memory, and he certainly showed that he was glad to see him by appointing him Adelantado, or Deputy Governor, of Hispaniola. As he was still confined to his bed, the arrival of his brother was a very fortunate thing, affairs in the colony being in a precarious and dangerous state.

When Ojeda and his army had reached Fort St. Thomas, Margarite, as ranking officer assumed the supreme command, and, leaving Ojeda with fifty men to garrison the fort, he set out, ostensibly to explore the island and intimidate Caonabo and other hostile chiefs. Instead of carrying out this plan, he descended to the fertile plain at the foot of the mountains, where he quartered his troops on the natives and began to enjoy himself. Following his example, the soldiers conducted themselves after the usual manner of idle and dissolute soldiers, and in a short time earned the enthusiastic hatred of the natives. Don Diego sent a remonstrance to Margarite, which that high-spirited gentleman regarded as an unwarrantable liberty. He refused to acknowledge Diego's authority, and, supported by his officers, set him at defiance. When it was evident that the patience of the natives would soon be exhausted, Margarite and some of his friends, including Father Boyle—who had become worn out by vainly waiting for an opportunity to experiment with a combustible heretic—seized one of the ships and sailed away to Spain.

The soldiers, being left without any commander, lost all organization, and the army melted away. The natives found steady and pleasant employment in killing them in small quantities at a time, and about a hundred of them took refuge with our old friend Guacanagari. Caonabo thought this would be a good opportunity for capturing Fort St. Thomas, and accordingly he besieged it with a large force, but after thirty days withdrew, completely baffled by the bravery of Ojeda and his handful of men. He then undertook to unite the caciques in a league against the Spaniards, and succeeded in inducing all of them to join him, with the exception of Guacanagari. The latter went to Isabella soon after Columbus arrived, and warned him that an overwhelming force was about to attack the city. Troops were sent out to attack the nearest of the hostile caciques, who was soon reduced to submission.

In the mean time, Ojeda with a small escort went to Caonabo's village and invited the cacique to visit Columbus and make a treaty with him, pledging him a safe-conduct. The cacique, weakly believing Ojeda's promise, accepted the invitation and started with a small army of followers. On the march Ojeda showed the cacique a pair of handcuffs, which he said were a decoration which the Spanish King conferred only on the most eminent of his subjects. Such, however, was the high opinion that the King had of Caonabo, that Ojeda was authorized to confer this splendid distinction upon him. As a preliminary, it would be necessary for Caonabo to mount on horseback, the bracelets being conferred only on mounted knights. Caonabo, feeling himself highly honored, climbed on Ojeda's horse, behind that astute officer, and submitted to be manacled. No sooner was this done than Ojeda, and his escort galloped away and brought the captive cacique to Isabella, where he was safely lodged in jail.

That Ojeda's conduct in this affair was treacherous and dishonorable there can be no question. Indeed, had he been the United States Government, and had Caonabo been a Black Hill Sioux, he could hardly have conducted himself more dishonorably than he did.

The native league was thus temporarily broken up, and the arrival of four ships from Spain, bringing, besides colonists and stores, a doctor and an entire apothecary's shop, gave Columbus strength enough to get out of bed before the doctor could begin operations on him. The King and Queen sent Columbus a letter, announcing that they took their several pens in hand to say that they were well and hoped Columbus was enjoying the same blessing, and that they had the utmost confidence in him. This letter completed the Admiral's cure, and he immediately organized an expedition against the natives, who were about to resume hostilities under the leadership of a brother of Caonabo.

Before setting out, he sent Diego back to Spain, ostensibly to look after his interests. Perhaps the true reason was that Diego was of very little use and was extremely unpopular. He was a well-meaning man, but his true sphere in life was that of a justice of the peace in Connecticut; and as Connecticut was not yet ready for him, Columbus thought he had better go home and wait until a good opening in East Lyme or Falls Village should present itself. At the same time, five hundred natives were sent to Spain to be sold as slaves, Columbus remarking that he hoped in this way to prepare their precious souls for the humanizing influence of the Gospel.

Having seen Diego safely started, Columbus, with Bartholomew, two hundred and twenty Spaniards, and twenty other bloodhounds, started to attack the savages. He met a hundred thousand of them—so the story goes—and defeated them with great slaughter. It is very probable that the number of the enemy was exaggerated, and that there were not more than ninety-nine thousand nine hundred and ninety-six, with perhaps two small-boys. There is no doubt, however, that they were shot down by the soldiers, ridden down by the horses, and mangled by the dogs to an immense extent, and that the battle was a glorious triumph of civilization over barbarism.

The victory was followed up by Columbus with energy. He marched through almost the entire length and breadth of the island, and compelled the caciques to make peace and pay a heavy tribute to the Spaniards. Every native was taxed either a certain amount of gold or its equivalent in cotton, according to Columbus's view of their relative value; and to secure his conquest, the Admiral built and garrisoned forts in different parts of the island, the most important of which was called Fort Concepcion, and was situated in the beautiful plain lying back of Isabella. Even Guacanagari and his people, who had remained faithful to Columbus, were taxed as heavily as the hostile natives, and that amiable cacique was so disgusted by this reward of his fidelity that he resigned his chieftainship and died of what in the case of a white monarch would be called a broken heart.

The yoke that the Spaniards had put on the native neck was too heavy to be borne. The savages resolved to starve their oppressors, and with this view destroyed their crops and retired to the mountains, to live on roots until the Spaniards should die of starvation. The plan was not successful. The Spaniards hunted the natives with dogs and dragged them back to work as slaves. Within a few months the free and happy people who had welcomed the Spaniards to the island, and were ready to worship them as superior beings, were converted into a horde of cowed and wretched slaves.

In later years, when Columbus had seen his own authority in Hispaniola set aside, and the island under the control of his rivals and enemies, he protested that the sight of the sufferings of the unhappy natives filled him with grief and horror. It was, however, to his political advantage at just that time to have his heart bleed for the poor savages, and the unprejudiced reader must regret that it did not bleed at an earlier period. It was under the immediate rule of Columbus that the natives of Hispaniola were first reduced to slavery, and it was Columbus who made his old friend and faithful ally, Guacanagari, suffer the same fate as the chiefs who had rebelled against the Spaniards. Then it cannot be forgotten that, in spite of the direct and repeated commands of Queen Isabella, Columbus sent cargo after cargo of slaves to Spain. He may have been very sorry to see the natives oppressed by Spaniards whom he disliked, but he certainly oppressed them quite as vigorously as did any of his successors. The contrast between his pious and humane protestations and his acts as an oppressor and a slave-trader is not easily explicable if we adopt the usual theory that he was one of the most sincere and noble of men. We may concede that he was naturally kind-hearted, and that he would have preferred gold-mining to slave-hunting; but when his interest urged him to cruelty, he usually listened to it with respectful attention, and straightway showed by his conduct that, although he was not a countryman of Ojeda and Pizarro, he was not altogether unfit to hold a Spanish commission.

CHAPTER XIV.

DIFFICULTIES AND DISCOURAGEMENTS.

MARGARITE and Father Boyle, as has been mentioned, had sailed for Spain while Columbus was absent on his cruise in search of China. Arriving in Spain, they told a series of able and effective falsehoods, judiciously seasoned with a little genuine truth. They said it gave them the greatest pain to speak in disparaging terms of their superior officer, but a stern sense of duty compelled them to say that the misguided man was a liar and a scoundrel. All the Admiral's stories of fertile islands, rich gold-mines, delightful climate, and amiable heathens clamoring for conversion, were without any foundation. Hispaniola was a wretched, fever-stricken place, wholly unfit for colonization. As for Columbus and his brother Bartholomew, they were cruel tyrants, who required Spanish gentlemen to work and made sick men get out of their beds, where they were comparatively comfortable, in order to engage in ridiculous expeditions after gold that never existed. Of the two, Don Bartholomew was perhaps the more objectionable, which was unfortunate, inasmuch as the Admiral, having put to sea in search of more of his worthless islands, had undoubtedly been drowned.

It must be confessed that, in one respect, Margarite and Boyle did tell the truth. There were chills and fever in the new colony, and when the King and Queen saw the returned colonists visibly shaking before them, they believed in the unhealthfulness of Hispaniola and all the accompanying lies told by the malicious and malarious complainants. They therefore resolved to send one Diego Carillo to Hispaniola as an investigating committee, to ascertain if there was anybody capable of telling the exact truth about the state of affairs.

But before Carillo could sail, Don Diego Columbus arrived, and as he brought considerable gold with him, the monarchs formed the opinion that he had the air of a man of strict veracity. He admitted that there was a part of the island of Hispaniola, a long distance from the colony, where it was said that chills and fever prevailed, and he was inclined to believe that the report was true. As for the climate of Isabella and its vicinity, he regarded it as exceptionally healthful. He reported that the Admiral had positively been to the mainland of China, and regretted that he had thoughtlessly forgotten to bring back confirmatory tea-chests.

Don Diego further assured the King and Queen that since the fortunate departure from Hispaniola of two objectionable persons whom he would not name, but who, he was informed, had recently arrived in Spain with a full cargo of assorted falsehoods, the affairs of the colony had been very prosperous. Of course, to bold and restless spirits there was a certain monotony in swinging in hammocks all day long, and eating delicious fruit, in a climate that was really perfect, and there were men who even grew tired of picking up nuggets of gold; but Don Diego was confident that, with a very few exceptions, the colonists enjoyed their luxurious life and, on the whole, preferred Hispaniola to Paradise.

Ferdinand and Isabella weighed the gold brought by Don Diego, and decided to believe him. They thereupon cancelled Carillo's appointment, and appointed in his place Juan Aguado, a personal friend of Columbus, who, it was understood, would go to Hispaniola in the character of a visiting statesman, and, after examining such witnesses as Columbus might introduce to him, would return home and make a report that would completely satisfy the Admiral.

In spite of this apparently friendly action, they gave Columbus just cause of complaint by throwing open the business of exploration, the monopoly of which they had formally given to him. They authorized any Spaniard to fit out exploring expeditions, under certain restrictions, and to discover continents, islands, and seas, without any limitation as to number; the discoverers to pay the Crown one third of all the gold they might find. Columbus was greatly grieved at this, not only because he feared that injudicious explorers would discover unhealthy islands, and would thus bring exploration into disrepute, but because it was a distinct breach of faith on the part of the King and Queen. As for the gracious permission which they gave him to freight a vessel to trade with the New World whenever any other explorer should freight one for the like purpose, he evidently did not trust himself to express his opinion of such a hollow mockery of his rights.

In August, 1495, Don Juan Aguado sailed for Hispaniola with a fleet loaded with supplies and a pocket filled with a royal decree, written on the best of parchment and ordering that the colony of

Isabella should consist of not over five hundred people. The astute monarchs had perceived that the larger the colony might be the more numerous and contradictory would be the complaints which the colonists would make, and hence they resolved to limit the complaint-producing capacity of the colony, and to render it impossible for more than five hundred distinct accounts of the infamy of Columbus and the climate to be brought to their royal ears.

As Aguado was supposed to be a firm friend of the Admiral, Don Diego Columbus decided to return with him to Isabella, which he accordingly did, arriving some time in October. We can imagine how glad Columbus must have been to find that his good though tedious brother's affection forbade him to desert his own dear Christopher. The latter was in the interior when Aguado arrived, and that officer immediately proceeded to astonish Don Bartholomew by putting on what Bartholomew rightly characterized as airs.

Aguado announced that he had come to put things to rights, and that the colonists now had a real friend to whom they could complain when insulted and oppressed by domineering Italians. As Isabella was undoubtedly a dull place, the colonists eagerly availed themselves of the new occupation of making complaints against Columbus and his brother, and displayed a promptness and industry of which they had never before given any signs. Don Bartholomew instantly sent word to his brother that a new and alarming kind of lunatic had arrived from Spain, with a royal commission authorizing him to raise the great adversary of mankind, and that the sooner the Admiral returned the better.

Columbus hastened to Isabella, where he greeted Aguado with such overwhelming politeness that the fellow became wretchedly unhappy. He had hoped to be able to report that Columbus had insulted him and treated the royal commission with contempt, but he was disappointed. He was a little cheered up, however, by a tremendous hurricane which wrecked all the Spanish ships except one, and kept the air for a time full of Spanish colonists, natives, and fragments of ruined buildings. This he thought would read very well in his intended report on the general infamy of the climate, and, despairing of obtaining anything better, he resolved to return to Spain as soon as a new vessel could be built. The Admiral announced that he intended to return with him, a piece of news that greatly discontented Aguado, who foresaw that after he had made his report concerning Columbus the latter would be entirely capable of making a report concerning Aguado.

About this time a young Spaniard arrived from the interior with a most welcome story. He had run away from Isabella on account of having nearly killed a fellow-colonist, and had met a beautiful female cacique living on the river Ozema, near the present site of San Domingo, who had fallen violently in love with him. From her he had learned of rich gold-mines, and he humbly trusted that Columbus would condescend to look at them and to overlook his little indiscretion in the matter of his fellow-colonist. The Admiral, secretly feeling that any man who killed one of his colonists was a benefactor of the human race, kindly forgave him and went with him to inspect the mines, which he found to be apparently so rich that he instantly overhauled his Old Testament and his Geography, and decided that he had found the original land of Ophir.

A new scientific person, who had been sent out to supersede the worthless Fermin Cedo, was ordered to take his crucibles, transit instruments, and other apparatus, and make a satisfactory assay of the mines. He did so, and, being a clever man, reported to the Admiral that the gold was unusually genuine, and that the ore would probably average three hundred dollars to the ton. At least, that is what he would have reported had he been a modern expert investigating mining property in behalf of British capitalists, and we need not suppose that there were no able assayers prior to the discovery of silver in Colorado. Columbus read the report, expressed a high opinion of the scientific abilities of the assayer, and ordered a fort to be built in the neigborhood of the mines.

Carrying with him specimens of gold from the new mines, and the report of the scientific person, Columbus sailed for Spain, in company with Aguado, on the 10th of March, 1496. He left Don Bartholomew as Governor during his absence, and took with him the captive chief Caonabo, either as a specimen of the kind of heathen produced by the island, or because he thought it might be possible to convert the chief with the help of the many appliances in the possession of the church at home. He wisely refrained from taking any slaves, Don Diego having informed him that the Queen had ordered his previous consignment of five hundred to be sent back to Hispaniola and set at liberty.

The homeward-bound fleet consisted of only two vessels, but they met with as much head-wind as if they had been a dozen ships of the largest size, and on the 10th of April they were compelled to stop at Guadaloupe for water and provisions. Here they were attacked by armed women as well as men. Several of these early American advocates of the equality of the sexes were captured, and set at liberty again when the ships sailed. One of them, however, improved the time by falling in love with Caonabo, whom she insisted upon accompanying, and Columbus consented to carry her to Spain as a beautiful illustration of the affectionate character of the Western heathen.

It was the 20th of April when the fleet left Guadaloupe, and Cadiz was not reached until the 11th of June. The provisions were so nearly exhausted that during the latter part of the voyage the sailors were almost in a state of starvation. Of course, when the provisions were scarce and the men were put on short allowance, the prisoner Caonabo and his affectionate female friend received their share of food, for Columbus would never have permitted the unfortunate pair to starve. Still, it did happen that Caonabo died on the voyage, and history is silent as to what became of his companion.

The returned colonists told dismal stories of their sufferings, but their stories were superfluous. Their wretched appearance; the way in which they clung to the lamp-posts and shook them till the glass rattled; and the promptness with which they rushed into the drug-stores and demanded—each for himself, in a single breath—"Six-dozen-two-grain-quinine-pills-and-be-quick-about-it!" furnished sufficient evidence of the sort of climate in which they had lived. It was useless for Columbus and his friends to say that the appearance and conduct of the shaking colonists were due to sea-sickness and long confinement on shipboard without proper provisions. The incredulous public of Cadiz could not be thus imposed upon, and the visible facts as to the colonists offset in the popular mind the magnificent stories of the mines of Ophir which the Admiral circulated as soon as he landed. The monarchs sent him a courteous invitation to visit the court, but he was in great doubt as to the kind of reception which Margarite, Father Boyle, and Aguado would prepare for him. In order to show that he felt himself greatly humiliated by the credence which had been given to the reports against him, he dressed himself in a Franciscan's coarse gown, and let his beard grow. On his way to court he paraded some thirty Indians whom he had brought with him, dressed principally in gold bracelets, and thereby created the false and alarming impression on the public mind that the Black Crook had broken out with much violence.

The King and Queen, when they saw the gold that Columbus had brought, and read the scientific person's certificates that it was genuine, decided to disregard all the complaints against the Admiral. Aguado had nothing to repay him for his long voyage, and no one would listen to his report. It is believed that he finally published it as an advertisement at so much a line in the local Cadiz paper, and sent marked copies to all his friends. If so, he benefited no one but the printers, and did Columbus no apparent injury.

Columbus was promised eight ships for a third exploring expedition, but the money was not in the treasury, or, at all events, the King and Queen could not make up their minds to spare it. They were engaged in two or three expensive wars and one or two difficult marriages, and were really quite pinched for money. At last, however, they gave Columbus an order for the amount; but before it was paid, Pedro Alonzo Niño, who had been sent with supplies to Hispaniola, returned to Cadiz and announced that his ships were filled with gold. The monarchs therefore recalled their order, and in its stead gave Columbus a draft on Niño, to be paid from his cargo of gold. Further investigation showed that Niño had spoken figuratively, and that he had no actual gold, but only a cargo of slaves, who, he estimated, would bring more or less gold if sold in the market.

Meanwhile the monarchs had appropriated all their ready money for purposes of slaughter and matrimony, and so were compelled to decline advancing funds for the new expedition until their business should improve.

Columbus had already lost much of his original popularity, and was daily losing what remained. That he had discovered new countries nobody denied; but the complaint was that he had selected cheap and undesirable countries. The Queen, however, still admired and trusted him, for the Admiral was a man of remarkably fine personal appearance. She confirmed all the previous honors and privileges that had been promised to him, which looks as if in those days a royal promise became outlawed, as the lawyers say, in one or two years unless it was renewed—a rule which must have greatly simplified the practice of diplomacy. Inasmuch as there had been a vast excess of expenses over receipts in the exploration business, Columbus was released from the obligation to pay an eighth of the cost of every expedition, and was given a large tract of land in Hispaniola, with the title of Duke, which title he refused, since it was inferior in rank to his title of Admiral.

While waiting for the expedition to be made ready, Columbus improved the time by making his will. In this document he committed the task of recovering the Holy Sepulchre to his son Diego, and directed him to save up his money by putting it in the savings bank, until he should have enough to pay for a crusade. Curiously enough, Don Diego never was able to accumulate the necessary sum, and the Holy Sepulchre is still waiting to be delivered. It was wise, however, in the Admiral to delegate this great duty to his son, and thus to free himself from an obligation which could not but interfere with the business of exploration. The more we can shift our burdens upon our descendants, the better time we shall have. This is the great principle upon which all enlightened nations base their financial policy.

Early in 1498 the royal business had so far improved that two vessels loaded with supplies were sent to Hispaniola, and preparations were made for fitting out a fleet of six ships and a force of five hundred men. The five hundred men were not easily found. It was the popular belief that chills and fever were not worth the trouble of so long a voyage, and that there was little else to be got by serving under Columbus. In this emergency, the sentences of criminals in the Spanish jails were commuted to transportation to the New World, and a pardon was offered to all persons for whom the police were looking—with the exception of heretics and a few other choice criminals—who should surrender themselves and volunteer to join the fleet. In this way the required number of men was gradually obtained. In point of moral character the expedition might have competed with an equal number of Malay pirates or New York plumbers. We are even told that some hardened and habitual musicians were thus carried by Columbus to the once peaceful and happy island of Hispaniola, taking with them their accordions and guitars. This is a blot upon the Admiral's character which his most ardent admirers cannot overlook.

CHAPTER XV.

HIS THIRD EXPEDITION.

THE perseverance of Columbus triumphed over all obstacles. The expedition was finally ready, and on the 30th of May, 1498, the Admiral went on board the flag-ship and, after remarking "All ashore that's goin'!" and "All aboard!" rang the final bell and started once more for the New World. Just as he was about to embark, one Breviesca, a clerk in the Indian Agents' Bureau, met him on the wharf and told Columbus that he would never return.

"What, never?" exclaimed the astonished Admiral.

"Well, hardly ever," replied the miscreant.

Of course Columbus instantly knocked him down, and went on board his vessel in a just but tremendous rage. He wrote to the Queen, informing her of the affair, and sincerely regretting that he had lost his temper. Long afterwards his enemies were accustomed to refer to the brutal way in which he had attacked an estimable and inoffensive gentleman, as a proof of his ungovernable temper, his Italian fondness for revenge, and his general unfitness for any post of responsibility.

The fleet steered first for Madeira, and then for the Canary Islands, touching at both places; and at the latter surprising—as historians assure us—a French privateer with two Spanish prizes. What there was about Columbus or his fleet that was so surprising, has, of course, been left to our imagination, in accordance with the habit of historians to omit mentioning details of real interest. The Frenchman was attacked by the Spaniards, but managed to escape together with one of his prizes. The other prize was retaken by the Spanish prisoners on board of her, and given up to Columbus, who turned the vessel over to the local authorities.

From the Canaries the fleet sailed to the Cape Verde Islands, where the Admiral divided his forces. Three ships he sent direct to Hispaniola, and with the other three he steered in a south-westerly direction, to make new discoveries. He soon discovered the hottest region in which he had ever yet been—the great champion belt of equatorial calms. There was not a breath of wind, and the very seams of the ships opened with the intense heat. It was evident to the sailors that they must be very close to the region where, according to the scientific persons of the period, the sea was perpetually boiling, and they began to fear that they would be roasted before the boiling process could begin. Luckily, a gentle breeze finally sprung up, and Columbus, abandoning the rash attempt to sail farther south, steered directly west, and soon passed into a comforting, cool, and pleasant climate.

On the 31st of July he discovered the island of Trinidad, and in view of the fact that his ships were leaky, his water almost gone, and his body alternately shaken by fever and twisted by gout, it was high time that land should have been found.

The following day the flag-ship was suddenly attacked by a canoe full of fierce natives, who threw spears and other unpleasant things at the Spaniards, and fought with great bravery. Columbus, determined to strike terror into the enemy, ordered his musicians to assemble on deck and play familiar airs—probably from "Pinafore." The result surpassed his most sanguine expectations. The unhappy natives fled in wild dismay as soon as the music began, and yelled with anguish when the first cornet blew a staccato note, and the man with the bass trombone played half a tone flat. When we remember that the good Queen Isabella had particularly ordered Columbus to treat the natives kindly, we must earnestly hope that this cruel incident never came to her presumably pretty ears.

The fleet was now off the south shore of Trinidad, and the mainland was in plain sight farther west. Columbus at first supposed that the mainland was only another island, and after taking in water he sailed west, with the intention of sailing beyond it. Passing through the narrow strait between Trinidad and the continent, he entered the placid Gulf of Paria, where to his astonishment he found that the water was fresh. Sailing along the shore, he landed here and there and made friendly calls on the natives, whom he found to be a pleasant, light-colored race, with a commendable fondness for exchanging pearls for bits of broken china and glass beads. No opening could be found through which to sail farther westward, and Columbus soon came to the opinion that he had this time reached the continent of Asia.

One thing greatly astonished him. He had been fully convinced that the nearer he should approach the equator the blacker would be the people and the hotter the climate. Yet the people of Paria were light-colored, and the climate was vastly cooler than the scorching regions of the equatorial calms. Remembering also the remarkable conduct of the stars, which had materially altered their places since he had left the Cape Verde Islands, and reflecting upon the unusual force of the currents which had latterly interfered severely with the progress of the ship, Columbus proceeded to elaborate a new and attractive geographical theory. He wrote to Ferdinand and Isabella that, in his opinion, the world was not exactly round, like a ball or an orange, as he had hitherto maintained, but that it was shaped like a large yellow pear. He assumed that the region which he had now reached corresponded to the long neck of the pear, near the stem, as it appears when the pear is resting on its larger end. He had consequently sailed up a steep ascent since leaving Spain, and had by this means reached a cool climate and found light-colored heathen.

This was a very pretty theory, and one which ought to have satisfied any reasonable inventor of geographical theories; but

Columbus, warming with his work, proceeded still further to embellish it. He maintained that the highest point of the earth was situated a short distance west of the coast of Paria, and that on its apex the Garden of Eden could be found. He expressed the opinion that the Garden was substantially in the same condition as when Adam and Eve left it. Of course a few weeds might have sprung up in the neglected flower-beds, but Columbus was confident that the original tree of the knowledge of good and evil, and the conversationally disposed animals, were all to be found in their accustomed places. As for the angel with the two-edged sword, who had been doing sentry duty at the gate for several thousand years, there could be no doubt that should an explorer present to him a written pass signed by the Pope, the angel would instantly admit him into the Garden.

Columbus now felt that, whatever failures might seem to characterize his new exploring expedition, he had forever secured the gratitude and admiration of the pious Queen. To have almost discovered the Garden of Eden in a nearly perfect state of repair was certainly more satisfactory than the discovery of any amount of gold would have been. Still, he thought it could do no harm to mention in his letter to the Queen that pearls of enormous value abounded on the coast, and that the land was fertile, full of excellent trees and desirable fruits, and populous with parrots of most correct conversational habits, and monkeys of unusual moral worth and comic genius.

Although Columbus failed to visit the Garden of Eden, either because he had no pass from the Pope or because he could not spare the time, it must not be imagined that he did not believe his new and surprising theory. In those happy days men had a capacity for belief which they have since totally lost, and Columbus himself was probably capable of honestly believing even wilder theories than the one which gave to the earth the shape of a pear and perched the Garden on the top of an imaginary South American mountain.

As the provisions were getting low, and the Admiral's fever was getting high—not to speak of his gout, which manifested a tendency to rise to his stomach—he resolved to cease exploring for a time, and to sail for Hispaniola. He arrived there on the 19th of August, after discovering and naming a quantity of new islands. The currents had drifted him so far out of his course, that he reached the coast of Hispaniola a hundred and fifty miles west of Ozima, his port of destination. Sending an Indian messenger to warn Bartholomew of his approach, he sailed for Ozima, where he arrived on the 30th of August, looking as worn out and haggard as if he had been engaged in a prolonged pleasure-trip to the Fishing Banks.

Don Bartholomew received his brother with the utmost joy, and proceeded to make him happy by telling him how badly affairs had gone during his absence. Bartholomew had followed the Admiral's orders, and had proved himself a gallant and able commander. He had built a fort and founded a city at the mouth of the Ozima, which is now known as San Domingo. Leaving Don Diego Columbus in command of the colony, he had marched to Xaragua, the western part of the island, and induced the Cacique Behechio and his sister Anacaona, the widow of Caonabo, to acknowledge the Spanish rule and to pay tribute. He had also crushed a conspiracy of the natives, which was due chiefly to the burning of several Indians at the stake who had committed sacrilege by destroying a chapel. These were the first Indians who were burnt for religious purposes, and it is a pity that Father Boyle had not remained in Hispaniola long enough to witness the ceremony which he had so often vainly urged the Admiral to permit him to perform. Probably Don Bartholomew was not responsible for the burning of the savages, for he evidently sympathized with the revolted natives, and suppressed the conspiracy with hardly any bloodshed.

The colonists, both old and new, were of course always discontented, and cordially disliked the two brothers of the Admiral. The chief judge of the colony, Francisco Roldan, undertook to overthrow the authority of the Adelentado, and to make himself the ruler of the island. After much preliminary rioting and strong language Roldan openly rebelled, and with his followers besieged Don Bartholomew in Fort Concepcion, in which he had taken refuge, and from which he did not dare to sally, not feeling any confidence in his men. Roldan was unable to capture the fort, but he instigated the natives to throw off Bartholomew's authority, and convinced them that he, and not the Adelentado, was their real friend.

The opportune arrival of the two supply ships, which sailed from Spain while Columbus was fitting out his third expedition, probably saved the authority and the life of Don Bartholomew. He immediately left the fort and, going to San Domingo, took command of the newly arrived troops, and proclaimed Roldan a traitor, which greatly relieved his mind. The traitor thereupon marched with his men to Xaragua, where they led a simple and happy life of vice and immorality. The discord among the Spaniards induced the natives to make another attempt to gain their liberty, but the Adelentado, in a brilliant campaign, once more reduced them to subjection. Two native insurrections, a Spanish rebellion, and unusual discontent were thus the chief features of the pleasant story with which Columbus was welcomed to Hispaniola.

Before he could take any active measures against Roldan, except to issue a proclamation expressly confirming Don Bartholomew's assertion that he was a traitor, the three ships which he had sent direct to Hispaniola when he divided his fleet at the Cape Verde Islands, arrived off the coast of Xaragua, and perceiving Spaniards on the shore, imagined that they were respectable colonists. Roldan fostered that delusion until he had obtained arms and supplies, when he admitted that from the holiest motives he had rebelled against the tyranny of the Adelentado.

The men of the fleet, learning that Roldan's followers were a set of reckless scoundrels, were inclined to think that perhaps transportation was not such a terrible affair after all, and began to desert with great alacrity, and to join the rebels. The ships therefore put to sea, and their commander, on arriving at San Domingo, informed Columbus that Roldan would probably surrender if it was made an object to him to do so.

The Admiral was anxious to march on Xaragua, capture Roldan, and make an example of him; but his unpopularity and that of his brothers was so great that he did not dare to risk leaving San Domingo, lest it should rebel as soon as his back was turned. In order to rid himself of some of the malcontents, he fitted out five vessels, and offered a free passage to Spain to every one who wished to return. The ships sailed, carrying letters from both

Columbus and Roldan, in which each described the other in uncomplimentary terms.

Columbus would now have marched against Roldan, but he could not find more than seventy men who felt well enough to march with him. The rest said they had headaches, or had sprained their ankles, and really must be excused. There was nothing left to do but to negotiate with the rebel leader, and compromise matters. Columbus began by offering a free pardon to Roldan if he would immediately surrender. Roldan, in his turn, offered to pardon Columbus if he would agree to certain conditions. These negotiations were continued for a long time, and after various failures the Admiral succeeded in obtaining a compromise. He agreed to reappoint Roldan Chief Judge of the colony; to grant him a certificate that all the charges which had been made against him were malicious lies; to give him and his followers back pay, slaves, and compensation for their property which had been destroyed; to send back to Spain such of the rebels as might wish to return, and to give the remainder large grants of land. On these conditions Roldan agreed to overlook what had passed and to rejoin the colony. This successful compromise served years afterwards as a model for Northern Americans when dealing with their dissatisfied brethren, and entitles Columbus to the honor of being the first great American compromiser.

Having thus settled the dispute, the Admiral wrote to Spain, explaining that the conditions to which he had agreed had been extorted by force and were therefore not binding, and that on Roldan's massive cheek deserved to be branded the legend *Fraud first triumphant in American History.* He asked that a commissioner should be sent out to arrest and punish the rebel chief, and to take the place of Chief Judge now fraudulently held by Roldan.

There is of course no doubt that Columbus would have hung Roldan with great pleasure had he been able to do so. He was compelled by force of circumstances to yield to all the rebel's demands, but nevertheless it was hardly fair for him to claim that his acts and promises were not binding. Still, it should be remembered that he was suffering from malarial fever, and it is notorious that even the best of men will tell lies without remorse if they live in a malarious region and have houses for sale or to let.

The Admiral, having thus restored order, was about to return to Spain to explain more fully his conduct and that of Don Bartholomew, when he heard that four ships commanded by Alonzo de Ojeda had arrived at Xaragua. He immediately suspected that something was wrong, and that in Ojeda he would have a new and utterly unscrupulous enemy to deal with. Foreseeing that an emergency was about to occur in which a skilful scoundrel might be of great assistance to him, he gave Roldan the command of two ships, and sent him to ascertain what

Ojeda intended to do. The wily Roldan anchored just out of sight of Ojeda's fleet, while the latter, with fifteen men only, was on shore. Landing with a strong force, and placing himself between Ojeda and his ships, he waited for the latter to meet him and explain matters.

Ojeda soon appeared, and was delighted to see a gentleman of whom he had heard such favorable reports. He said he was on his way to San Domingo, and had merely landed for supplies. He had been authorized to make discoveries by Fonseca, the Secretary of Indian Affairs, and his expedition had been fitted out with the assistance of Amerigo Vespucci and other enterprising merchants. He had been cruising in the Gulf of Paria, and had his ships loaded with slaves. As soon as he could he intended to visit Columbus, who, he regretted to say, was probably the most unpopular man in Spain, and would soon be removed from his command. Roldan returned to San Domingo with this information, and both he and the

Admiral agreed that they did not believe anything that Ojeda had said.

Meanwhile Ojeda, having met with many of Roldan's former adherents, who still lingered in Xaragua, was informed by them that Columbus had not given them their back pay. Ojeda said that such injustice made his blood boil, and that if they would join him he would march to San Domingo and put an end to the base Italian tyrant. The new rebellion was prevented by the arrival of Roldan with a respectable array of troops, and Ojeda promptly went on board his flag-ship. Roldan wrote to him asking for an interview, and reminding him that rebellion was a crime which every good man ought to abhor. Ojeda, replied that such was precisely his opinion, and he must refuse to have anything to do with a man who had lately been a rebel.

Soon afterward Ojeda sailed away in a northerly direction, keeping near the shore, and Roldan marched along the coast to intercept him in case he should land. Arriving at a place called by the natives Cahay, Ojeda sent a boat ashore, which was captured by Roldan, and in order to regain it he was finally forced to consent to parley with his antagonist. The result was that Ojeda promised to sail immediately for Spain. Having made this promise he naturally landed soon after on another part of the island, but being followed by Roldan he finally abandoned Hispaniola and sailed for Cadiz with his cargo of slaves.

The Admiral was greatly pleased at this signal illustration of the wisdom of the proverb about setting a rogue to catch a rogue, and writing Roldan a complimentary letter, requested him to remain for a little while in Xaragua.

While Ojeda's ships were at Xaragua, Columbus had passed sentence of banishment on Hernando de Guevara, a dissolute young Spaniard, and sent him to embark on board one of Ojeda's vessels. He arrived at Xaragua after the ships had left, and Roldan ordered him to go into banishment at Cahay. Guevara, however, had fallen in love with an Indian maid, the daughter of Anacaona, and wanted to remain in Xaragua and marry her. Roldan would not listen to him, and the unhappy youth went to Cahay, where he stayed three days and then returned. There was a spirited quarrel between him and Roldan, and the latter finally yielded and allowed Guevara to remain.

The grateful young man immediately conspired against Roldan and the Admiral. He had a cousin, De Mexica, a former associate of Roldan's in rebellion, who immediately took up the cause of the exile. De Mexica soon convinced his ex-rebel friends that the spectacle of Roldan, as an upright, law-abiding man, was simply revolting, and that he and Columbus ought to be killed. He had gathered a small force together, when he and his chief associates were suddenly surprised by the Admiral, arrested, tried, and hanged before they had time to realize that anything was the matter.

Don Bartholomew was dispatched to Xaragua to aid Roldan, and the two, after arresting Guevara, stamped out the new rebellion with remorseless energy. This time there was no compromise, and a suspicion began to prevail that rebellion was not so safe and profitable an industry as it had been hitherto.

CHAPTER XVI.

HIS RETURN IN DISGRACE.

ON the 23d of August, 1500, two ships arrived at San Domingo, commanded by Don Francisco de Bobadilla, who had been sent out by the Spanish monarchs as a commissioner to investigate the state of the colony. The enemies of Columbus had at last succeeded in prejudicing Ferdinand and Isabella against him. Ojeda, the returned colonists, Roldan's rebels, and the letters of Roldan himself, all agreed in representing the Admiral as a new kind of fiend, with Italian improvements, for whom no punishment could be sufficiently severe.

Ferdinand calculated the total amount of gold which Columbus had either carried or sent to Spain, and, finding it smaller than he had expected, could no longer conceal his conviction that Columbus was a cruel, tyrannical, and wicked man. Isabella had hitherto believed in the Admiral, and had steadily stood by him while under fire, but in face of the evidence which had latterly been submitted to her, and in view of the cargo of slaves that had been sent from Hispaniola to Spain in spite of her orders, she was compelled to admit that an investigation should be made, and sanctioned the appointment of Bobadilla, with the understanding that he would let no guilty man escape.

The average historian is always very indignant with the monarchs for sending Bobadilla to San Domingo, and regards that act as a wanton persecution of a great and good man. But the cold and sceptical inquirer will ask how it happened that every person who came under the Admiral's authority, with the exception of his two brothers, invariably made complaints against him. It is true that the majority of the colonists were men whose word was unworthy of credit, but had Columbus been a just and able ruler, surely some one outside of his own family would have spoken favorably of him. We need not suppose that he was responsible for the chills and fever which harassed the colonists, or that he originated all the hurricanes and earthquakes that visited the island; but there is sufficient reason to believe that he was not well fitted to win the obedience or respect of the colonists, and in the circumstances we may restrain our indignation at the appointment of the investigating commissioner.

Ferdinand and Isabella evidently had cofidence in the judgment and integrity of Bobadilla, for they gave him three or four different commissions, with authority to use any or all of them, as he might see fit. As the event proved, he was unworthy of this confidence; but it would not be fair to accuse the monarchs of deliberate cruelty because they overrated their commissioner's intelligence.

Bobadilla arrived at San Domingo just after the suppression of Mexica's rebellion, and while Columbus was still absent at Fort Concepcion. As he entered the river he saw two gibbets decorated with rebel corpses, and the sight was not adapted to remove the impression, which he undoubtedly had, that Columbus was cruel and tyrannical.

His first act was to publish a proclamation that he had come to redress grievances, and that every one in San Domingo who had any cause of complaint against Columbus or his brothers should at once speak out, or ever after hold his peace. The entire population, with the solitary exception of those who were locked up in jail, at once hastened to Bobadilla and told their grievances.

The commissioner, appalled at the flood of accusation which he had set loose, strengthened his mind by attending mass, and then caused his commission appointing him to inquire into the late rebellion to be read. This having been done, he demanded that Don Diego Columbus, who was in command of San Domingo, should surrender to him Guevara and the other rebel prisoners. Don Diego said that he held the prisoners subject to the Admiral's order, and must therefore decline to surrender them. Bobadilla next produced a second commission appointing him Governor of the New World, and remarked that perhaps Don Diego would now condescend to give up the prisoners. Don Diego conceded that the commission was a very pretty one, especially in point of seals and ribands, but maintained that his brother had a better one, and that, on the whole, he must decline to recognize Bobadilla as Governor. Exasperated by this obstinacy, Bobadilla now produced a third commission, ordering the Admiral and his brothers to surrender all the forts, public buildings, and public property to him, and forcibly argued that since Guevara was in a fort, the surrender of the fort would include the surrender of Guevara, in accordance with the axiom that the greater includes the less. Don Diego calmly insisted that this was not a case in which mathematics were concerned, and that he proposed to obey the Admiral's orders, no matter if Bobadilla should keep on producing new commissions at the rate of sixty a minute for the rest of his natural life.

Bobadilla, finding that Don Diego's obstinacy was proof against everything, went to the fort and called on the commander to give up his prisoners, and when the commander refused, broke into the fort, at the head of the delighted colonists, and seized on Guevara and his rebel companions. He then took possession of all the property and private papers belonging to the Admiral, and, moving into his house, proceeded to assume the duties of Governor and investigator.

Columbus, when he heard of these proceedings, was somewhat astonished, and remarked to his friends that he feared this Bobadilla was a little rash and impolitic. He wrote to him, welcoming him to the island, and suggesting that it would be well if he were to draw it mild—or words to that effect. In reply, Bobadilla sent him an order to appear before him at once, and enclosed a letter from the sovereigns, ordering Columbus to obey the combined Governor and Commissioner in all things. Being wholly without means of resistance, Columbus perceived that magnanimity was what posterity would expect of him, and therefore immediately went to San Domingo and presented himself before Bobadilla.

That amiable and delicate person received the Admiral as if he were an Italian brigand for whom a reward of $25,000 had been offered, and ordered him and his brother, Don Diego, to be put in irons, As a striking instance of the irony of fate, it may be mentioned that the man who placed the irons on Columbus was his former cook, whose self-respect had often been wounded when his master complained that the maccaroni was burned or that the roast pork was insufficiently cooked. Now the cook had his revenge, and we can imagine with what zest he remarked, after the fetters were riveted, that he hoped that for once the Admiral would admit that the job was well done, and would notice the rare pleasure with which his ex-cook had performed it, whatever might have been that humble but honest individual's previous sins in respect to pork and maccaroni. Undoubtedly he said something of the kind, for a man who could put chains on Columbus was surely bad enough to make puns without shame or remorse. At the command of Bobadilla, Columbus wrote to Don Bartholomew, who was in Xaragua, inviting him to come and share the fetters of his illustrious brother and the well-meaning Don Diego —which the Adelantado accordingly did.

Having the entire Columbus family thus safely in his power, Bobadilla procceded to take testimony against them, with all the enthusiasm of a partisan Senate committee preparing material for a Presidential campaign. There was no lack of testimony. The colonists made affidavits with a wealth of imagination and fervency of zeal which a professional detective employed to furnish evidence in an Indiana divorce case might emulate but could not surpass. Columbus was accused of nearly all modern and ancient crimes, from stealing pearls and gold-dust up to the crowning infamy of requiring Spanish gentlemen to work. It was conclusively shown that he was the worst man then living, with the possible exception of the Adelentado, and that Guevara and the other rebels were patent, direct-acting saints, who deserved every possible honor. Having made up an effective campaign document from this mass of brilliant testimony, Bobadilla sent it, together with Columbus and his two brothers, to Spain.

Don Alonzo de Villejo, who commanded the vessel on board of which was the fallen Admiral, was a gallant sailor, and, as soon as the ship was safely out of the harbor, said, in the strongest seafaring language, that he would consent to the immediate condemnation of his personal eyes if the Admiral should wear those doubly condemned chains another moment. But Columbus courteously and firmly refused to be liberated. He said the chains had been put on him by order of the King and Queen, and that the King and Queen would have to take them off, or he would wear them to his dying day, and serve them right. This was a stout-hearted resolution, but, perhaps just to gratify Villejo, Columbus consented now and then to slip one wrist out of his fetters, which he must have found very inconvenient when he was engaged in writing letters.

The voyage was uneventful, and in the early part of October the ship reached Cadiz and Columbus was delivered to the local authorities. The moment it was known that he had been brought home in irons he became immensely popular, as indeed the man who made so unexpected and brilliant a sensation deserved to be. Everybody said it was an outrage, and that Bobabilla was clearly the beast spoken of in the Apocalypse.

Columbus did not venture to write to the Queen, but he wrote a long and eloquent account of his bad treatment to one of the ladies of the court, who he knew would instantly read it to Isabella. That estimable sovereign was greatly shocked, and Ferdinand felt that, as a prudent husband, he must share his wife's indignation. The royal pair immediately wrote a letter expressing the warmest sympathy for Columbus, inviting him to court, and enclosing a check for nearly $8500 to pay his travelling expenses and enable him to buy a few clean collars and other necessaries.

The Admiral, taking off his chains and putting them in his trunk as souvenirs of royal favor, went to Granada, where the court was then held, and being admitted to the royal presence fell at the feet of Isabella, which he appears to have carefully distinguished from Ferdinand's feet, and burst into tears. The monarchs personally raised him up, in spite of his weight, and Isabella told him it was a perfect shame, and that Bobadilla's conduct was quite too awfully horrid. Ferdinand behaved very properly, and agreed with

Isabella that all the rights and honors of Columbus should be restored to him, and that he could feel perfectly easy as to the future. Bobadilla's elaborate campaign document was tossed aside with as little attention as if it had been a Patent Office Report, and his attempt to fire the royal Spanish heart was a complete failure.

Columbus now expected that he would be directed to return immediately to San Domingo, and to send Bobadilla home in disgrace; but the monarchs delayed to issue the desired orders. Ferdinand had evidently made up his mind to do nothing of the sort. He considered himself a deeply injured king. In the confident expectation that Columbus would be drowned, he had consented to grant him unprecedented honors and privileges, in the improbable contingency of the discovery of a new road to Asia or a new continent. Columbus had meanly taken advantage of this to discover a continent and innumerable islands, and had, as Ferdinand felt, cheated him out of a splendid title and a handsome revenue. Now that Columbus had temporarily lost these ill-gotten advantages, Ferdinand did not think it necessary to restore them. He therefore informed the Admiral that it would be best for him to remain in Spain for, say, ten years, until things could be made pleasant for him in Hispaniola. In the mean time Don Nicholas de Ovando would be sent out to supersede Bobadilla nd to ascertain what damages Columbus and his brothers had sustained, so that full payment could be made. He assured the Admiral that everything should be arranged to his satisfaction, and that he should lose nothing by remaining in Spain.

There is no reason to suppose that Columbus was deceived by the King's attenuated explanation, but he could not well find fault with it. De Ovando sailed for San Domingo with a fleet of thirty vessels and twenty-five hundred men. Columbus took lodgings in Granada, and to employ his time resolved to attend to the little matter of recovering the Holy Sepulchre, a duty which he had long neglected and had recently bequeathed to his son. He drew up a long memorial, urging the King and Queen to organize a new crusade for the capture of Jerusalem. He demonstrated to his own satisfaction that he had been born in order to discover a new world and to redeem the Holy Sepulchre. He had fulfilled the first of these duties, and was now ready for the second. All that he required was an army and a sufficient supply of money.

Ferdinand did not embrace the suggestion with much enthusiasm. He said he would see about it, and hinted that as crusading was an expensive business, it might be well to ascertain whether the Sultan would be willing to look at the matter from a business point of view and make some arrangement in regard to the Holy Sepulchre which would settle the matter in an amicable and inexpensive way.

The crusading scheme being a failure, the Admiral devised a new plan of exploration. He wrote another memorial, setting forth the advantages of discovering the Panama Canal. He admitted that either China had been moved, or else it lay farther west of Spain than he had at first supposed. At any rate, it had become clear to his mind that there was a continent which blocked up the direct route to China, and that the only way to get through this obstacle was to discover a canal *à niveau*, cutting the Isthmus of Panama. He had not the least doubt that the canal was there, and that he could find it with perfect ease were he to be supplied with ships and men, and were a proper reward to be offered for its discovery. Now that he had time for reflection, he was inclined to think the market had latterly been overstocked with new countries—a result which he had feared when the sovereigns so injudiciously—if he might be allowed the expression—gave to everybody the privilege of exploration. In regard to the Panama Canal, however, he was confident that it would meet a great public want, and that its discovery would be warmly applauded by everybody, with the possible exception of the inhabitants of Bohemia, who, although they had no commerce, might insist that the canal should not be discovered unless the discoverer would agree to present it to them.

The plan pleased Ferdinand and Isabella. A fleet of four ships was ordered to be made ready, and Columbus was authorized to take with him his brother Don Bartholomew and his personal son, Diego. The monarchs also wrote Columbus a letter, in which they said many pleasant and inexpensive things, and promised him the restoration of all his rights. He was now so enfeebled by age and hardship that it seemed safe to promise him anything, provided the promises were not to be fulfilled until after his return from his intended voyage.

CHAPTER XVII.

HIS FOURTH EXPEDITION.

ON the 9th of May, 1502, Columbus once more sailed from Cadiz. The passage across the Atlantic was in no way remarkable. The fleet touched as usual at the Canaries, and on the 15th of June arrived at one of the smaller Caribbean islands. Columbus had been strictly forbidden to touch at San Domingo, because it was feared that he would get into trouble with the local authorities, and would then come back to Spain to defend himself against false accusations. However, as one of his ships was unseaworthy, he convinced himself that it was a matter of necessity and mercy for him to go to San Domingo and obtain a better vessel.

He arrived in due time at the forbidden port, but Ovando refused to permit him to land, and ordered him to put to sea immediately. Columbus then informed Ovando that a hurricane was approaching, and begged permission to lie at anchor in the shelter of the harbor until fair weather should appear; but his petition was refused. Ovando said there was not the least sign of an approaching hurricane, and that he was a bird far too advanced in years to be caught by the Admiral's meteorological chaff.

There was at the time a large fleet of vessels lying in the harbor, and on the point of sailing for Spain. On board of the fleet were Roldan, Bobadilla, many discontented colonists, and a large quantity of gold. Now Columbus, who was learned in weather, was in earnest when he prophesied a hurricane, and he felt sad in view of the danger which threatened the gold on board the fleet in case the ships should put to sea before the hurricane arrived. He warned Ovando not to let the fleet depart, but Ovando and everybody else laughed to scorn "Old Italian Probabilities," and mocked at his areas of barometrical depression and approaching storm-centres.

Columbus sailed away and sought shelter under the lee of the island, and the fleet with Bobadilla and the gold put to sea. Two days later a hurricane that the New York *Herald* would have been proud to launch against the shores of Great Britain wrecked the fleet, drowned Bobadilla and Roldan, and sunk the gold to the bottom of the sea. A few vessels managed to work their way back to San Domingo, but only one reached Spain. The fortunate vessel had on board a quantity of gold belonging to Columbus, and in his opinion this fact was all that saved her.

The Admiral's vessels rode out the storm safely, though they were much damaged, and, after it was over, put into Port Hermoso to refit. Having patched up the vessels, Columbus set sail for the Panama Canal, and after a voyage of about six weeks he reached a group of small islands on the coast of Honduras. Here he met a large canoe filled with the ablest natives he had yet seen. They had hatchets and other tools made of copper, and were dressed in cotton garments woven by themselves. They were probably from Yucatan, for they claimed to belong to a civilized country situated farther west and possessing magnificent cities. The Admiral said he was not looking for cities as much as he had been, that he was on his way to India, and that he had no time to go to Yucatan. Thus he lost the chance of discovering the curious and fantastic Maya and Aztec civilization which Cortez afterward found and destroyed.

There was little in the early part of the Admiral's voyage along the Central American coast which deserves especial notice. He coasted Honduras and Costa Rica, finding an oppressive sameness of savages and bad weather. The savages were peaceful, but the weather was not. It rarely condescended to indulge in anything less violent than a hurricane, and always blew from precisely the direction in which the Spaniards wished to steer. The Costa Rican savages told Columbus that the Ganges was a few days' journey farther west, and that vessels carrying cannons frequently came to the large city of Ciguari, which was still nearer than the Ganges.

This was, on the whole, the most able and satisfactory aboriginal lie which had yet been told to Columbus, and it made him confident that he would arrive in India in a few days. Lest the savages should receive too much credit for inventive genius, it should be mentioned that they must have been greatly assisted by leading questions put by the Spaniards, otherwise they could not have hit upon the name of the Ganges. The mention of the ships armed with cannon which came to the mythical city of Ciguari was, however, a masterstroke for which the natives are entitled to full credit. Travellers who have visited Central America in our day would perhaps find it easier to understand the habits and customs of the people, were it generally known that their remote Indian ancestors were likewise men of brilliant imagination and utter fearlessness of assertion.

Leaving these mendacious but encouraging savages, Columbus came to Veragua, a country lying farther south and really abounding in gold. But now that he had finally reached a place where gold was abundant, the precious metal for which Columbus had searched so long and eagerly seemed to have lost its charm. He was too anxious to reach the Ganges to be willing to stop for anything; so, after laying in a few gold plates, he stood on his southward course.

The ships and the Admiral were by this time greatly in want of repairs. Columbus was suffering from gout, fever, and old age, while the ships, in addition to the latter complaint, were leaky and covered with barnacles. The crews began to grumble loudly, and on the 5th of December, Columbus having failed to find the Ganges, the city of Ciguari, or the Panama

Ship-Canal, thought it best to yield to the force of public opinion before it should express itself with handspikes and knives. He therefore consented to abandon his search and turn back to Veragua, where he hoped to be able to collect enough gold to convince Ferdinand and Isabella of his wisdom in postponing his intended geographical discoveries.

No sooner had the ships turned and stood to the northward, than the wind, with a vicious display of ill-temper, shifted and became once more a head-wind. It blew if anything harder from its new quarter than it had blown before, and it was not until early in January that the fleet reached Veragua and anchored in the river Belen.

The sailors were glad to go ashore; for, though there was nothing to drink, there was gold to be got, and while on shore they were rid of the task of sailing clumsy and leaking ships. The Admiral, in his feeble health, was greatly in need of rest, and he was not aware that he had found precisely the worst locality in the Western

Hemisphere for fever and mosquitoes. The Adelentado was sent with a large force to explore the surrounding country, from which he returned with the report that the natives had a great deal of gold in their possession. Of course the Spanish soldiers merely looked at this gold, and complimented the natives on their possession of so valuable an article; we need not suppose they were so wicked as to steal it, and thus convert the friendly Costa Ricans into enemies.

Being satisfied with the Adelentado's report, Columbus decided to leave most of his men to found a colony on the banks of the Belen, while he should return to Spain for supplies.

The natives had hitherto been peaceable; but when they saw the Spaniards building houses on their land, they felt that it was time to take proceedings for dispossession. Columbus received information that the local cacique, Quibian, was collecting an army to attack the colony, and he sent Diego Mendez to investigate the matter.

Quibian's village was on the river Veragua, not far from the Belen, and Mendez soon found his way thither. He was told that the cacique was confined to his house with a wounded leg. Mendez immediately said that he was a doctor, and would repair the leg; but Quibian's son said, Oh no, he rather thought Mendez would not repair that particular leg just then. As the savage followed up this remark by hitting Mendez over the head, the latter admitted that perhaps he was mistaken, and hurriedly remembered that he had an engagement which would require his immediate return to the colony.

There was now no doubt that Quibian intended to fight, and the Adelentado, remarking that a cacique in the hand was better than several in the bush, proposed to go in person and capture Quibian. Taking seventy-four men with him, Don Bartholomew managed to obtain an interview with the cacique, whom he instantly seized and bound. The natives offered no resistance, and the Adelentado, gathering up the wives and children of Quibian, prepared to return.

The cacique was laid in the bottom of a boat, and pretended to suffer so much pain that the officer in charge of the boat loosened his bonds. Quibian thereupon jumped overboard and, as it was now night, escaped safely to land; while the Spaniards believed that he had been drowned.

The danger of an attack by the savages being thus, in the opinion of the Admiral, at an end, he prepared to depart for Spain. The water on the bar at the mouth of the river was so low that the ships could not pass over it without being lightened. Their stores were therefore disembarked, and after getting into deep water the ships were anchored and the stores were brought back to them in boats.

When the fleet was nearly ready to sail, Columbus sent Diego Tristan and eleven men ashore to obtain water. As they neared the settlement, they saw a horde of savages rush out of the jungle and attack the colonists. The savages were led by

Quibian, who, being a heathen and a barbarian, imagined that he had more right to his wives and children than the Spaniards had. Tristan was an excellent old sailor, who held that it was the first duty of man to obey orders. He had been sent for water and not for blood, and accordingly he never thought of interfering in the fight, but rowed steadily up the river in search of fresh water. The Spaniards fought bravely, and repulsed the attack of the natives; but the latter, instead of appreciating Tristan's fidelity to duty, fell upon him and killed him and his whole party, with the exception of one man, who fled to the settlement with his sanguinary story.

The Spaniards were now convinced that they had no more use for Central America, and rushed to the ship that lay in the river, determined to return to Spain with the Admiral. The ship, however, could not be got over the bar, and the terrified colonists consented to listen to the Adelentado's advice, and to attempt to fortify the settlement. They went on shore again, and threw up barricades—which, as every one knows who is familiar with French politics, consist of boxes, paving-stones, omnibuses, news-stands, and other heterogeneous articles piled together.

The barricades were better than nothing as defensive works, but they were miserably weak. Eleven Spaniards had been killed and several more wounded, including Don Bartholomew, and as the savages vastly outnumbered them, the prospect that any of the colonists would escape was extremely small.

Columbus could not understand why Tristan did not return. He knew that Tristan was a faithful and obedient man, and that there was no rum to be had at the settlement, so that he finally began to fear that the natives had been acting in a disorderly way. This fear was increased by the conduct of Quibian's wives and children, who were on board one of the vessels. During the night after Tristan's departure these hasty and ill-bred prisoners began to commit suicide by hanging themselves or by jumping overboard, and continued this recreation so persistently that by morning not one of them was left. If women and children could do such an uncivil thing as this, it was only too probable that the men of the same race were capable of creating riot and bloodshed ashore.

There was only one available small boat at the command of the Admiral, and the sea on the bar was so heavy when the disappearance of the Quibian family was discovered that Columbus did not dare to send the boat ashore. Fortunately, one of the pilots, Pedro Ledesma, offered to swim ashore if the boat would carry him part of the way. His offer was of course accepted, and when the boat was a short distance from the shore Ledesma sprang overboard and successfully swam through the boiling surf. He returned in a short time, bringing the news that the colonists were in immediate danger of being massacred.

Unless the sea should go down, Columbus could give no assistance to the men on shore, and there was no prospect that the sea would go down.

Most men in the position of the Admiral would have been at a loss what to do, but Columbus was a man of uncommon resources. He promptly had a vision. A voice spoke to him in the best Scriptural style, and assured him that everything was all right; that the colonists would be saved, and that no one need feel any uneasiness. It is probable that this was the voice of a sainted and remote ancestor of the late William H. Seward, and it filled the Admiral with confidence—which confidence it is possible was shared by the sailors when the story of the vision was told to them. The voice proved to be a veracious one, for the next morning there was a dead calm, and the colonists, with all their portable property, were safely rafted on board the ships, which immediately set sail for San Domingo in order to refit.

It was now the end of April, but the weather declined to improve. Probably Columbus, like a skilful commander, made his men draw lots with a view to pilgrimages, and encouraged them to vow to attend church in their shirts; but there is no mention of these manœuvres in the Admiral's log. The ships were nearly eaten up by the teredo and could with difficulty be kept afloat. One was abandoned, and the crew taken on board the other two. These reached the islands lying south of Cuba which Columbus had discovered on his second voyage, where they were detained nearly a week by violent storms. When the voyage was resumed the head-winds promptly resumed also, and finally, with his ships leaking like sieves out of repair, and his provisions nearly exhausted, Columbus bore up for Jamaica, which he reached on the 23d of June. The next day he entered the harbor of Port Santa Gloria, where his decrepit vessels were run ashore to keep them from sinking, and were firmly lashed together.

CHAPTER XVIII.

HIS LAST YEARS.

THE ships were now hopeless wrecks, and there was nothing more to be done with them except to abandon them to the underwriters and claim a total loss. The only chance that the Spaniards could avoid laying their bones in the bake-ovens of the Jamaican natives was in communicating with San Domingo, but in the absence of any efficient postal service this chance seemed very small. Diego Mendez, who was the captain of one of the vessels, and who had earned the confidence of Columbus by the skill with which he superintended the escape of the beleagured colonists from Quibian's hordes, volunteered to take a canoe and, with the help of Indian paddlers, make his way across the one hundred and twenty miles of sea which stretched between Jamaica and Hispaniola. He started on his voyage, and skirted the shore of Jamaica, so that he could land from time to time and take in provisions.

It struck the natives that they might as well improve the opportunity to lay in provisions for themselves, and accordingly they attacked Mendez with great energy and appetite, and made him and his Indian paddlers prisoners. There being in all seven prisoners, a dispute arose as to the fairest way of dividing them, and the savages agreed to settle it by a game of chance —which was probably "seven-up." Mendez took advantage of the quarrelling to which the game gave rise, and ran away. At the end of a fortnight he appeared before the Admiral and announced that all was lost except honor and his canoe.

The bold Mendez was not disheartened, but volunteered to make a second attempt. This time he was joined by Fresco, the captain of the other wreck, together with twelve Spaniards and twenty Indians. The expedition started in two large canoes, and the Adelentado, with an armed force, marched along the shore as far as the extreme eastern point of the island to protect the canoes from any attack by the natives. Mendez and his companions suffered terribly from exposure and thirst, and many of the Indian paddlers died—a fact which shows either that the Spaniards could endure thirst better than the Indians, or that the latter had less water to drink than the former.

The expedition finally reached Hispaniola, having formed a very low opinion of canoeing as an athletic sport. According to the original plan, Mendez was to induce Ovando to send a ship to Columbus, and Fresco was to return with the news that Mendez was at San Domingo, hard at work inducing the Governor to send the ship; but as the surviving Indian paddlers said they were satiated with paddling and did not intend to return to Jamaica, Fresco was compelled to remain in Hispaniola.

Ovando, hearing that Columbus was in

Jamaica, thought he had better stay there, and instead of sending a vessel to his relief, constantly promised to do so at the earliest possible moment, and constantly took good care that no such moment should arrive.

Meanwhile the shipwrecked men were becoming very discontented. When a man has nothing to do but to think of what he is to have for dinner, and then never has it, he is reasonably sure to exhibit a fretful spirit. This was the condition of the Spaniards at Port Santa Gloria. They were living on board the wrecked vessels because they did not care to tempt the appetites of the natives by living on shore; and as the Admiral was confined to his cabin with the gout, and could not overhear them, they naturally relieved their minds by constantly abusing him, one to another.

Francesco de Porras, who had been a captain of one of the ships—and it really seems as if there were as many captains in proportion to the size of the fleet as there are in the United States navy—thought this was a favorable time for mutiny, and accordingly proceeded to mutiny. He reminded the men that Columbus was unpopular in Spain, and was forbidden to land in San Domingo. This being true, why should he ever leave Jamaica, where he had nothing to do except to lie in his cabin and enjoy the pleasures of gout? He insisted that Mendez and Fresco would never return, and that they were either drowned or had gone to Spain. In short, by lucid arguments such as these he convinced the crews that Columbus intended to keep them in Jamaica for the rest of their lives.

Having thus induced the crews to mutiny, Porras went into the Admiral's state-room and demanded that he should instantly lead the Spaniards back to Spain. Columbus took the ground that this was an unreasonable demand, since an ocean voyage could not be successfully made without vessels; but Porras, disgusted with such heartless quibbling, rushed on deck and called on his followers to embark in canoes and start for Cadiz without a moment's delay. His proposal was enthusiastically received, and a tumult ensued which brought the crippled Admiral on deck on his hands and knees, in the vain hope of enforcing his authority.

It was hardly to be expected that in such an attitude he could strike the mutinous sailors with awe. Indeed, the probability that they would strike him instead was so great that the Adelentado had his brother carried back to the cabin, and there stood on guard over him as coolly as if he were not at the mercy of an armed mob.

The mutineers, to the number of fifty, seized on a fleet of canoes and started for Spain by way of San Domingo. Twice they were driven back, and the second time they gave up the attempt. They then wandered through the island, robbing the natives and alleging that they were very sorry to do so, but they were acting under express orders from Columbus, and that, as disinterested friends of the noble Jamaicans, their advice was that the Admiral should be killed without delay.

Weeks and months passed by, and no word came from Mendez and Fresco. The natives, finding the Spaniards at their mercy, made a corner in provisions and refused to sell except at an exorbitant price. Thus famine began to threaten the unfortunate explorers. It was then that Columbus performed his celebrated eclipse feat. He summoned the caciques, and told them that in view of the enormity of their conduct it had been decided to withdraw the moon from heaven, and that this purpose would be carried out at the end of three days. The Admiral had, of course, looked into his Public Ledger Almanac, and had noticed that a total eclipse of the moon, visible throughout the Gulf States and the West Indies, would take place on the night in question.

When the third night came, and the eclipse began, the Indians were terribly frightened, and begged the Admiral to forgive them and give them back their beloved moon. At first he refused to listen to them, but when the eclipse reached its period of greatest obscuration he relented, and informed them that, for the sake of the young men and young women of Jamaica, to whom the moon was almost indispensable, he would give them one more chance. The natives, overwhelmed with gratitude, and determined not to lose the moon if they could help it, brought all the provisions that the Spaniards wanted.

This was the first instance of turning American celestial phenomena to practical uses; but the example of Columbus has since been followed with great success by our scientific men, who induce the government to send them at vast expense to all parts of the world, under the plausible pretext of superintending total eclipses and transits of Venus.

Mendez had been gone eight months when a small vessel entered the harbor where the shipwrecked vessels were lying. It carried Don Diego de Escobar, bearer of despatches from Ovando to Columbus. Ovando wrote promising to send a ship to rescue Columbus and his companions as soon as he could find one suitable for the purpose. Having delivered this message and received an answer, De Escobar instantly sailed away, to the immense disgust of everybody. He was not altogether a nice person, having been one of Roldan's gang whom Bobadilla had released from prison. The Admiral could not help thinking that it was hardly delicate in Ovando to select such a messenger, but it was still a satisfaction to know that Mendez had reached San Domingo, and that in the course of a few years Ovando might find it convenient to send the promised ship.

Columbus now thought it was a good time to offer an amnesty to Porras and his companions, on condition that they would return to duty. Porras rejected the offer with disdain. He informed his men that it was only a trap set by the wily Italian to get them once more in his power. When they timidly suggested that a messenger from Ovando had really visited the Admiral, and that this looked as if negotiations were in progress for the purpose of arranging for the rescue of the expedition, Porras boldly insisted that the alleged messenger and the vessel in which he was said to have arrived had no existence. They were simply "materialized" by Columbus, who was a powerful spiritual medium, and they had already vanished into thenothingness from which they had been called.

Convinced by this able address, the mutineers decided to remain under the leadership of Porras, who immediately marched with them to attack the Admiral and to seize the stores that still remained. Don Bartholomew met them, and after a hard fight completely defeated them, taking Porras prisoner. The survivors gladly surrendered, and Columbus magnanimously forgave them.

In June, 1503, two ships arrived from San Domingo. One had been fitted out by Mendez, and the other by Ovando, who saw that Columbus would be rescued, and that he might as well earn part of the credit therefor. The Spaniards hurriedly embarked, and on the 23d of the month, after a stay of more than a year in Jamaica, they sailed for San Domingo, where they arrived after a voyage of about six weeks. Ovando professed to be exceedingly glad to meet the Admiral, and told him that for the last six or eight months he had been steadily occupied in wasting to a mere shadow, so anxious had he been to find a favorable moment for deciding upon the propriety of sending a vessel to the rescue of his distinguished friend. Columbus received his explanation with politeness, remarking " Ha !" and also " Hum !" at appropriate intervals, just to intimate that, while he did not care to argue with Ovando, he was not quite so credulous as some people imagined. The populace were disposed to overlook their bad treatment of their former Governor, inasmuch as his arrival at San Domingo was an interruption of the monotony of their life; so they cheered him when he passed through the street, and gave the old man the last glimpse of anything like popularity which he was to see.

Columbus was not anxious to remain long in the island. His business affairs were in an intricate state of confusion, and though a large sum of money was due to him, he could not collect it. The condition of the Indians filled him with grief. Under the rule of Ovando they had been constantly driven to revolt by oppression, and then mercilessly massacred, while the Spanish priests had expended a great deal of firewood and worn out several full sets of controversial implements, such as racks and thumbscrews, in converting them to Christianity. Columbus saw that his discovery of Hispaniola had led to the ruin and misery of its people, and he could not remain in any comfort amid so much suffering. Porras had already been sent as a prisoner to Spain, and on September 12th Columbus followed him. Ovando had supplied two vessels, one commanded by Columbus and the other by Don Bartholomew, but one of them was soon sent back as being unseaworthy. After a stormy voyage the ship arrived at San Lucas on November 7th, and the sick and crippled Admiral was carried to Seville, where he intended to rest before proceeding to court.

This time he was not received with any enthusiasm. He had so often returned from voyages to China without bringing with him so much as a broken tea-cup as a sample of the Celestial Kingdom, that the public had lost all interest in him. People who read in their newspapers among the list of hotel arrivals the name of Columbus, merely remarked, " So he's back again it seems," and then proceeded to read the criticism upon the preceding night's bullfight. The popular feeling was, that Columbus had entirely overdone the matter of returning home from profitless explorations. There were other explorers who came back to Spain with stories much more imaginative than those which Columbus could tell, and the Spanish public had turned its attention from Prester John and the Emperor of China to the Amazonian warriors of South America and the Fountain of Youth which explorers of real enterprise were ready to discover.

Had there been any knowledge of the science of politics in Spain, Columbus would have been a person of considerable importance in his old age. The Radicals would have rallied around him, and would have denounced the atrocious manner in which a treacherous and reactionary monarchy had treated him. Columbian clubs would have been established everywhere, and he would have been made to serve as the stalking-horse of an unprincipled and reckless faction.

When we compare the way in which the Italian republicans have used the name and fame of Garibaldi as the most effective weapon in striking at the monarchy which has made United Italy possible, we cannot but despise the ignorance of politics shown by the Spaniards in the beginning of the sixteenth century.

Columbus, though utterly worn out, was still able to write letters. He wrote to the King, to the Queen, to everybody who had any influence, asking that his honors and privileges should be restored, and hinting that he was ready to be sent back to San Domingo as Governor. No one paid any attention to him. Other men were fitting out exploring expeditions, and Columbus, with his splendid dreams and his peculiar mixture of religion and geography, was regarded as a foolish old man who had outlived his original usefulness. He was too sick to visit the court and personally explain why he had not discovered the Panama Canal, and the King, having failed to keep his own promises, was naturally not at all anxious to see him. Perhaps Isabella would have still remained faithful to her old protégé, but she was on her deathbed, and died without seeing him.

In May, 1505, Columbus managed to go to Segovia, where Ferdinand held his court. He saw the King, but got very little pleasure thereby. Ferdinand was now a widower and his own master; and his manner plainly showed Columbus that, whatever the King might promise, he never intended to keep his word and do justice to the man who had given him a new world.

The end was now drawing near, and Columbus made a codicil to his will, expressing his last wishes. Beatrix Enriquez was still alive, though whether she too had forsaken Columbus we are not told. It is pleasant to find that the Admiral remembered her, and in the codicil to his will ordered his son Diego to see that she was properly cared for, adding, "and let this be done for the discharge of my conscience, for it weighs heavy on my soul." He had neglected to marry Beatrix, and, unlike most men in like circumstances, the neglect burdened his conscience. This codicil was almost the last act of his busy life; and on the 20th of May, 1506, repeating the Latin words, *In manus tuas, Domine, commendo spiritum meum*, he died with the calmness of a brave man and the peace of a Christian. He had lived seventy years, and had literally worn himself out in the service of the royal hound whose miserable little soul rejoiced when he heard that the great Italian was dead.

Columbus was buried almost as much as he was born. His first burial was in the convent of St. Francisco. Seven years later he was buried some more in the Carthusian convent in Seville. In 1536 he was carried to San Domingo and buried in the Cathedral, and afterward he was, to some extent, buried in Havana. Whether Havana or San Domingo has at present the best claim to his grave, is a disputed point.

CHAPTER XIX.

HIS CHARACTER AND ACHIEVEMENTS.

HITHERTO we have proceeded upon the assumption that Columbus was a real historical person. It is one of the limitations of biography that the writer must always assume the existence of the subject of his sketch. There are, however, grave reasons for doubting whether Christopher Columbus ever lived. There is the matter of his birthplace. Is it credible that he was born in seven distinct places? Nobody claims that George Washington was born in all our prominent cities, or that Robinson Crusoe, who was perhaps the most absolutely real person to be found in the whole range of biography, was born anywhere except at York. Can we believe that the whole of Columbus was simultaneously buried in two different West Indian cities? If we can accept any such alleged fact as this, we can no longer pretend that one of the two Italian cities which boast the possession of the head of John the Baptist is the victim of misplaced confidence.

And then the character of Columbus as portrayed by his admiring biographers is quite incredible, and his alleged treatment by the King and Queen whom he served is to the last degree improbable. The story of Columbus is without doubt an interesting and even fascinating one; but can we, as fearless and honest philosophers, believe in the reality of that sweet Genoese vision—the heroic and noble discoverer of the New World?

There are strong reasons for believing that the legend of Christopher Columbus is simply a form of the Sun myth. We find the story in the Italian, Spanish, and English languages, which shows, not that Colombo, Colon, and Columbus ever lived, breathed, ate dinner, and went to bed, but that the myth is widely spread among the Indo-Germanic races. Columbus is said to have sailed from the east to the west, and to have disappeared for a time beyond the western horizon, only to be found again in Spain, whence he had originally sailed. Even in Spain, he was said to have had his birthplace in some vague locality farther east, and to have reached Spain only when near his maturity.

This is a beautiful allegorical description of the course of the sun as it would appear to an unlearned and imaginative Spaniard. He would see the sun rising in the distant east, warming Spain with his mature and noonday rays, setting beyond the western horizon in the waters of the Atlantic, and again returning to Spain to begin another voyage, or course, through the heavens. The clouds which at times obscure the sun are vividly represented by the misfortunes which darkened the career of Columbus, and his imprisonment in chains by Bobadilla is but an allegorical method of describing a solar eclipse. The colonists who died of fever under his rule, like the Greeks who fell under the darts of the Sun God, remind us of the unwholesome effects produced by the rays of a tropical sun upon decaying vegetation; and the story that Columbus was buried in different places illustrates the fact that the apparent place of sunset changes at different points of the year.

There is very much to be said in favor of the theory that Columbus is a personification of the Sun, but that theory cannot be accepted either by a biographer or by any patriotic American. The one would have to put his biography of the Great Admiral in the fire, and the other would lose all certainty as to whether America had ever been discovered. We must resolve to believe in the reality of Columbus, no matter what learned sceptics may tell us; and we shall find no difficulty in so doing if we found our belief on a good strong prejudice instead of reasonable arguments.

Let us then permit no man to destroy

our faith in Christopher Columbus. We can find fault with him if we choose; we can refuse to accept Smith's or Brown's or Jones's respective estimates of his character and deeds: but let us never doubt that Columbus was a real Italian explorer; that he served an amiable Spanish Queen and a miserable Spanish King; and that he sailed across a virgin ocean to discover a virgin continent.

There prevails to a very large extent the impression that the voyages of Columbus prove that he was a wonderfully skilful navigator, and it is also commonly believed that the compass and the astrolabe were providentially invented expressly in order to assist him in discovering America. There was, of course, a certain amount of practical seamanship displayed in keeping the *Santa Maria* and her successors from being swamped by the waves of the Atlantic; but it may be safely asserted that only a very slight knowledge of navigation was either exhibited or needed by Columbus. The ships of the period could do nothing except with a fair wind. When the wind was contrary they drifted slowly to leeward, and when the wind was fair a small-boy with a knowledge of the elements of steering could have kept any one of them on her course. The compass was a handy thing to have on board a ship, since it gave to the sailors the comfortable feeling which an ignorant man always has in the presence of any piece of mechanism which he fancies is of assistance to him; but for all practical purposes the sun and the stars were as useful to Columbus as was his compass with its unintelligible freaks of variation. So, too, the astrolabe must have impressed the sailors as a sort of powerful and beneficent fetish, but the log-book of Columbus would have testified that the astrolabe was more ornamental than useful.

The system of navigation followed by Columbus was to steer as nearly west as practicable on the way to America, and to steer as nearly east as possible on his way back to Spain. In the one case he would be sure to hit some part of the New World if he sailed long enough, and in the other case persistent sailing would be sure to bring him within sight of either Europe or Africa. In neither case could he so far overrun his reckoning as to arrive unexpectedly at some point in the interior of a continent. The facts prove that this was precisely the way in which Columbus navigated his ship. When steering for America he never knew where he would find land, and was satisfied if he reached any one of the countless large and small West India islands; and on returning to Spain there was as much probability that he would find himself at the Azores or at the mouth of the Tagus as at any Spanish port.

The truth is, that neither the seamanship of Columbus nor the invention of the compass or the astrolabe made his first voyage successful. Probably any one of the thousands of contemporary Italian sailors could have found the West Indies as easily as Columbus found them, provided the hypothetical sailor had possessed sufficient resolution to sail westward until the land should stop his way. What we should properly be called upon to admire in Columbus as a navigator of unknown seas is the obstinacy with which he adhered to his purpose of sailing due west until land should be found, no matter if it should take all summer. It was an obstinacy akin to that with which our great Union General fought his last campaign. Such obstinacy will sometimes accomplish greater results than the most skilful navigator or the profoundest strategist could accomplish. Had the man who discovered our country or the man who saved it been less obstinate, American history would have been widely different from what it has been.

As the astrolabe has been mentioned several times in the course of this narrative, it may be well to describe it, especially as it is now obsolete. It was an instrument of considerable size, made of some convenient material—usually either metal or wood, or both—and fitted with various contrivances for the purpose of observing the heavenly bodies. When a navigator took an observation with the astrolabe he immediately went be lowand "worked it up" with the help of a slate and pencil, and in accordance with the rules of arithmetic and algebra. The result was a series of figures which greatly surprised him, and which he interpreted according to the humor in which he happened to find himself. A skilful navigator who could guess his latitude with comparative accuracy generally found that an observation taken with the astrolabe would give him a result not differing more than eighty or ninety degrees from the latitude in which he had previously imagined his ship to be, and if he was an ingenious man he could often find some way of reconciling his observation with his guesses. Thus the astrolabe gave him employment and exercised his imagination, and was a great blessing to the lonesome and careworn mariner.

It is our solemn duty, as Americans, to take a warm interest in Christopher Columbus, for the reason that he had the good taste and judgment to discover our beloved country. Efforts have frequently been made to deprive him of that honor. It has been urged that he was not the first man who crossed the Atlantic, that he never saw the continent of North America, and that he was not the original discoverer of South America. Most of this is undoubtedly true. It is now generally conceded the Norwegians landed on the coast of New England about six hundred years before Columbus was born; that Americus Vespuccius was the first European to discover the South American continent; that Sebastian Cabot rediscovered North America after the Norwegians had forgotten all about it; and that Columbus never saw any part of what is now the United States of America. For all that, Columbus is properly entitled to be called the discoverer of the New World, including the New England,

Middle, Gulf, Western, and Pacific States. Who invented steamboats? And who invented the magnetic telegraph? Every patriotic American echo will answer, "Fulton and Morse." There were nevertheless at least four distinct men who moved vessels by machinery driven by steam before Fulton built his steamboat, and nearly twice that number of men had sent messages over a wire by means of electricity before Morse invented the telegraph. The trouble with the steamboats invented by the pre-Fultonians, and the telegraphs invented by the predecessors of Morse, was that their inventions did not stay invented. Their steamboats and telegraphs were forgotten almost as soon as they were devised; but Fulton and Morse invented their steamboats and telegraphs so thoroughly that they have stayed invented ever since.

Now, the Norwegians discovered America in such an unsatisfactory way that the discovery came to nothing. They did not keep it discovered. They came and looked at New England, and, deciding that they had no use for it, went home and forgot all about it. Columbus, who knew nothing of the forgotten voyage of the Norwegians, discovered the West India islands and the route across the Atlantic in such a workmanlike and efficient way that his discoveries became permanent. He was the first man to show people the way to San Domingo and Cuba, and after he had done this it was an easy thing for other explorers to discover the mainland of North and South America. He thus discovered the United States as truly as Fulton discovered the way to drive the *City of Rome* from New York to Liverpool, or Morse discovered the method of sending telegrams over the Atlantic cable.

We need not be in the least disturbed by the learned men who periodically demonstrate that Leif Ericson, as they familiarly call him, was the true discoverer of our country. We need never change " Hail Columbia" into " Hail Ericsonia," and there is not the least danger Columbia College will ever be known as Leifia University. We can cheerfully admit that Leif Ericson—or, to give him what was probably his full name, Eliphalet B. Ericson—and his Norwegians landed somewhere in New England, and we can even forgive the prompt way in which they forgot all about it, by assuming that they landed on Sunday or on a fast-day, and were so disheartened that they never wanted to hear the subject spoken of again. We can grant all this, and still cherish the memory of Columbus as the true and only successful discoverer of America.

Most biographers have written of Columbus in much the same way that a modern campaign biographer writes the life of the Presidential candidate from whom he hopes to receives an office. They forget that he was never nominated by any regular party convention, and that it is therefore wrong to assume, without any sufficient evidence, that he was the greatest and best man that ever lived. He was undoubtedly a bold sailor, but he lived in an age when bold sailors were produced in quantities commensurate with the demands of exploration, and we cannot say that he was any bolder or better sailor than the Cabots or his own brother Bartholomew. He was certainly no braver soldier than Ojeda, and his conquests were trifling in comparison with those of Cortez and Pizarro.

As a civil ruler he was a conspicuous failure. It is true that the colonists over whom he was placed were, many of them, turbulent scoundrels; but the unanimity with which they condemned his administration, and the uniformity with which every commissioner appointed to investigate his conduct as a ruler condemned him, compel us to believe that he was not an able governor either of Spanish colonists or contiguous Indians. He was not habitually cruel, as was Pizarro, but he insisted upon enslaving the Indians for his own profit, though Queen Isabella had forbidden him to enslave them or to treat them harshly.

He could be magnanimous at times, but he would not undertake a voyage of discovery except upon terms which would ensure him money and rank, and he did not hesitate to claim for himself the reward which was offered, during his first voyage, to the man who should first see the land, and which was fairly earned by one of his sailors.

As an explorer, he failed to find a path to India, and he died under the delusion that Pekin was somewhere in Costa Rica. His first voyage across the broad Atlantic seems to us a wonderful achievement, but in either difficulty or danger it cannot be compared with Stanley's march across the African continent. We must concede to Columbus a certain amount of boldness and perseverance, but we cannot shut our eyes to the faults of his conduct and character.

And yet Columbus was a true hero. Whatever flaws there may have been in the man, he was of a finer clay than his fellows, for he could dream dreams that their dull imaginations could not conceive. He belonged to the same land which gave birth to Garibaldi, and, like the Great Captain, the Great Admiral lived in a high, pure atmosphere of splendid visions, far removed from and above his fellow-men. The greatness of Columbus cannot be argued away. The glow of his enthusiasm kindles our own, even at the long distance of four hundred years, and his heroic figure looms grander through successive centuries.

THE END.

INDEX.

Aguado, Juan, appointed investigator, 185; investigates, 188; makes nothing by it, 195.

Angel, Luis de St., 56; offers to advance money, 57.

Astrolabe, invented, 32; description of, 276.

Black Crook, thought to have broken out in Spain, 194.

Bobadilla, Francisco de, arrives in Hispaniola, 221; arrests Columbus, 228; sends Columbus to Spain, 229.

Boyle, Father Bernardo, 133; desires to burn somebody, 150, 163; is disappointed, 174.

Caonabo, 160; captured, 175; dies, 193.

Cedo, Fermin, alleged scientific person, 158.

Cogoletto, alleged birth-place of Columbus, 1.

Columbus, Bartholomew, born and translated, 4; is sent to England, 38; arrives at Hispaniola, 171; made Governor of Isabella, 191; able commander, 209; arrested, 228; sails with fourth exploring expedition, 236; defeats Porras, 261.

Columbus, Christopher, born, 1; translated, 3; anecdotes of boyhood, 5; goes to Pavia, 9; becomes sailor, 11; engages in Neapolitan expedition, 12; deceives sailors or posterity, 13; does not arrive in Portugal, 16; does arrive there, 18; marries, 19; makes maps, 20; lives at Porto Santo, 21; goes to Iceland or elsewhere, 28; talks to King John, 35; goes to Spain, 38; deposited with Quintanilla, 41; meets Scientific Congress, 43; goes to Convent of Rabida, 49; meets committee on exploration, 54; starts for France, 56; goes to Palos, 61; sails on first voyage, 67; keeps false reckoning, 56; discovers San Salvador, 89; sails for Spain, 97; wrecked, 102; founds colony, 105; sees Mermaids, 110; displays seamanship, 115; arrives at Azores, 116; arrives at Palos, 125; flattens egg, 135; sails on second voyage, 138; discovers Dominica, 141; returns to Spain, 191; loses popularity, 196; sails on third voyage, 200; discovers Trinidad, 204; invents ingenious the-

ory, 205 ; arrives at Hispaniola, 208 ; arrested, 228 ; sent to Spain, 229 ; arrives in Spain, 230 ; sails on fourth voyage, 237 ; reaches Honduras, 240 ; searches for Panama Canal, 240 ; founds colony at Veragua, 243 ; sails away, 250 ; reaches Jamaica, 251 ; manages lunar eclipse, 258 ; reaches Hispaniola, 262 ; returns to Spain, 264 ; dies, 268 ; is extensively buried, 268 ; perhaps is a sun-myth, 269; character, 284.
Columbus, Diego, born, 4 ; Governor of Isabella, 162 ; sent to Spain to wait for opening in Connecticut, 177; returns to Hispaniola, 187 ; arrested by Bobadilla, 227.
Columbus, Dominico, combs wool, 3.
Compass, variation of, 55.
Congress of Salamanca, 46 ; its tediousness, 45.
Correo, Pedro, 21; he winks, 25 ; is talked to death, 34.

Enriquez, Beatrix, loves not wisely but too well, 41 ; is mentioned in Columbus's will, 267.
Ericson, Eliphalet B., discovers America, 281.
Eclipse, story of, 258.
Egg, story of, 135.

Ferdinand, King of Aragon, 40.

Guacanagari, his affection for Columbus, 101 ; his suspicious leg, 150 ; falls extensively in love, 152 ; protects Spaniards, 175.

Isabella, Queen of Castile, 41.

John, King of Portugal, 29 ; his dishonorable conduct, 34.

La Navidad, founded, 105 ; destroyed, 148.
Ledesma, Pedro, swims ashore, 249.

Marchena, Juan Perez de, prior of a convent, 50 ; makes a night of it with Columbus, 51.
Margarite, rebels, 174.
Mendez, Diego, tries to reach Hispaniola from Jamaica, 252 ; succeeds, 254.
Mendoza, Cardinal de, gives dinner, 135.
Mexica, De, rebels, 219.

Ojeda, Alonzo de, is a just man, 158; captures Caonabo, 175 ; arrives at Xaragua, 215 ; his interview with Roldan, 216.
Ovando, Nicholas de, sent to Hispaniola, 233 ; refuses to let Columbus land, 237 ; delays to send aid to Columbus 255 ; finally does send it, 262.

Perestrello, Mrs., mother-in-law of Columbus, 20 ; her use of the stove-lid, 21.
Pinzon, Martin Alonzo, fits out ship to join Columbus,

56 ; has a brilliant idea, 83 ; deserts, 97 ; met by Columbus, 108 ; reaches Palos, 127 ; displays good sense, 128.

Pinzon, Vincente Yanez, fits out ship to join Columbus, 56.

Porras, Francisco de, mutinies, 256 ; defeated and captured, 261.

Prester John, who he was, 31 ; who he was not, 166.

Quibian, attacks colony, 246

Quintanilla, receives Columbus on deposit, 41.

Roldan, Francisco, rebels, 210; compromises, 215; outwits Ojeda, 216 ; drowned, 239.

Ships, rigged by Indianians, 64.

Talavera, De, the Queen's confessor, 43.

Triano, De, discovers land, 86 ; is disgusted.

Villejo, Alonzo de, risks his eyes, 229.

www.ingramcontent.com/pod-product-compliance
Lightning Source LLC
Chambersburg PA
CBHW032058220426
43664CB00008B/1056